THE PRACTITIONER GUIDE TO PARTICIPATORY RESEARCH WITH GROUPS AND COMMUNITIES

Kaz Stuart and Lucy Maynard

With forewords by
Deborah Terras and Lonnie Rowell

First published in Great Britain in 2023 by

Policy Press, an imprint of
Bristol University Press
University of Bristol
1–9 Old Park Hill
Bristol
BS2 8BB
UK
t: +44 (0)117 374 6645
e: bup-info@bristol.ac.uk

Details of international sales and distribution partners are available at
policy.bristoluniversitypress.co.uk

© Bristol University Press 2023

British Library Cataloguing in Publication Data
A catalogue record for this book is available from the British Library

ISBN 978-1-4473-6227-2 paperback
ISBN 978-1-4473-6228-9 ePub
ISBN 978-1-4473-6229-6 ePdf

The right of Kaz Stuart and Lucy Maynard to be identified as authors of this work
has been asserted by them in accordance with the Copyright, Designs and Patents
Act 1988.

All rights reserved: no part of this publication may be reproduced, stored in a
retrieval system, or transmitted in any form or by any means, electronic, mechanical,
photocopying, recording, or otherwise without the prior permission of Bristol
University Press.

Every reasonable effort has been made to obtain permission to reproduce copyrighted
material. If, however, anyone knows of an oversight, please contact the publisher.

The statements and opinions contained within this publication are solely those of the
authors and not of the University of Bristol or Bristol University Press. The University
of Bristol and Bristol University Press disclaim responsibility for any injury to persons
or property resulting from any material published in this publication.

Bristol University Press and Policy Press work to counter discrimination on grounds of
gender, race, disability, age and sexuality.

Cover design: Liam Roberts Design
Front cover image: iStock/seb_ra
Bristol University Press and Policy Press use environmentally
responsible print partners.
Printed and bound in Great Britain by CMP, Poole

Contents

List of figures and tables

Figures

Tables

Glossary

Anonymity	the process of disconnecting data from individual names or identities so it is not possible to know who said or thought what.
Arts-based data collection tools	using drawing, art, dance, drama, sculpting, modelling or any other arts or creative tool to collect data.
Audiences	the audience/s for your research is the people who you want to read it and use it. It could include people at all levels of society.
Coding	this is the process of giving different names to the different groups of data you collect together.
Communication channel	this refers to the way you communicate with your audience. It includes things such as letters, phone calls, emails, social media and so on. Some will be more suited than others to reaching your audience.
Concept map	a visual diagram of related ideas on a topic.
Confidentiality	keeping a name or identity out of the public domain so no one knows who participated in the research.
Constructivism	a research philosophy based on the idea that people construct reality and truth together in how they converse, think and act.
Content analysis	a process of analysing the content of images or words to draw out meanings.

Context statement	this presents other people's views on the research topic as a backdrop to what you are doing.
Co-researchers	people who design or do research with one another as experts by experience.
Creative data collection tools	see arts-based data collection tools.
Cultural competence	the ability to communicate and act in ways which are appropriate to the culture of the people you are working with.
Data	the numbers, words or images you end up with as a result of conducting your research.
Data analysis	the way in which you find patterns of meaning in the data in order to come up with a final message/s.
Data collection tools	the things you use to collect data – there are lots of these, for example surveys, focus groups and interviews.
Data protection	keeping data safe and secure and ensuring participants know how their data will be used and stored.
Digital data collection tools	collecting data with people using a range of online tools such as social media, email and collaborative platforms.
Discourses	the different voices about your research topic, for example government, media and researchers.
Dissemination strategy	identifying who you want to communicate your research to, what format they will pay attention to and how to get that in front of them to ensure your research has maximum impact.
Equal	everything being the same or divided up on an equal basis.
Equity	some people having more support than others in order for their access to resources and opportunities to be the same.

Evaluation	a process by which someone decides how 'good' a project was. It can also be referred to as a review.
Focus groups	a research method that brings together a group of people to collect data on their discussion of a particular topic.
Government policy	policies produced by governments which state what must be done and guide how things are done nationally.
Graphic illustrator	someone who can bring ideas to life in a picture.
Grey literature	this refers to everything published that is not a policy, law, media report, research paper or theoretical literature. This often includes reports by organisations or opinion pieces.
Incentive	a financial or 'in kind' payment for participation in a research project.
Informed consent	the process of an individual or group agreeing to take part in a research project after they have been informed of what will be involved.
Interpretivism	a research philosophy that is another name for post-positivism and means that people interpret things in different ways and so values different people's views of the world.
Interviews	a conversation designed to collect in-depth data from a small number of participants.
Knowledge democracy	ensuring everyone can generate knowledge in ways that are meaningful to them, rather than knowledge being created by a privileged few in ways that suit them.
Law	the legal framework which mandates how things are done and what the consequences of breaking the law are.

Literature review	this is a process of collecting, reviewing and summarising all the key pieces of writing on your research topic.
Literature search strategy	this is a statement that explains what literature you will search for and what you will exclude from the search.
Locating your study	this means working out how your views and findings sit amongst the other voices (government, media, other researchers) on this topic.
Mapping tools	participants using diagrams and maps to answer the research questions.
Media	newspapers, TV and online news providers. Each may have a different view depending on their political views.
Narratives	a story that someone tells about themselves in response to a research question.
Opportunity sampling	asking anyone relevant that you know if they want to take part in your research.
Paradigms	a set of beliefs about the role of research. Different research philosophies have different paradigms. Also called a world view.
Participant information form	a written document providing the person taking part in the research with all the information about what will be expected of them and what will happen with their data.
Participatory methods	ways of conducting research that enable engagement and characterise it as participatory.
Participatory research	doing research 'with' people as active contributors to the research process, rather than doing research 'on' people.
Photovoice	a participant taking a set of photos and then talking about them.
Positivist research	research that aims to prove things (for example, experiments).

Post-positivist research	research that aims to explore things (for example, lived experience).
Primary data	data you have collected yourself.
Purposive sample	deciding on a list of people to ask who meet the criteria for your research group.
Qualitative analysis	tools to analyse words and images (coding and thematic analysis).
Qualitative research	research that collects words, images and sounds as data.
Quality measures	the beliefs you have about what 'quality' research is and the practical steps you take to ensure your research is of high quality.
Quantitative analysis	tools to analyse numbers (statistical analysis).
Quantitative research	research that measures (quantifies) things, using numbers as data.
Random sampling	randomly asking anyone who is eligible to take part in the research.
Recruitment strategy	a plan to think through how to best engage people in your research.
Remuneration	financial payment for time working in a research project.
Research aim	the overall purpose and boundaries of the research project.
Research alignment	the degree to which the different stages of research match one another.
Research dissemination strategy	a fancy way of saying: who will you share your research with and how?
Research ethics	a set of principles to keep everyone safe and to help make sure your research will not unintentionally harm anyone.
Research message	the meaning you want people to hear or read in your research outputs.
Research method	the type of research you will use – like a research recipe.

Research methodology	a set of beliefs about research, reality, trust and knowledge that forms a logical framework for how the research is done (the same meaning as philosophy).
Research output	the end product of your research – a report, film, play or art display.
Research participants	the people who take part in your research, either providing data or taking part in the whole research project.
Research philosophy	a set of beliefs about research, reality, truth and knowledge that underpin and guide how research is done (the same as research methodology).
Research purpose	what you want to achieve from your research project (the same as a research aim).
Research questions	the questions that will help your research purpose.
Right to withdraw	every participant should be able to withdraw from the research and should know how to do so.
Running ethics	the process of thinking about and solving ethical issues throughout a research project rather than just at the start.
Sampling strategy	a plan to ensure you engage the 'right' group of people in your research.
Secondary data	using existing data to answer a research question.
Snowball sampling	asking a small group of relevant people to take part in your project, and also asking them to find another one or more participants so the participants grow like a rolling snowball.
Social justice	a world where everyone has equitable support and equal access to resources and opportunities.
Statistical analysis	tools to analyse numbers.

Stratified sampling	asking people from certain groups who are eligible whether they want to take part in your research.
Surveys	a set of questions used to collect data from lots of participants.
Target population	the group of people who would all be eligible to take part in your study.
Thematic analysis	tools to analyse words and images.
Theoretical literature	academic papers and books which state a theory without drawing on research data.
Transcription	the process of writing or typing out audio and visual data so you have a written record of everything that was said.
Verbatim	writing something exactly as it was said.
Visual analysis	tools to analyse images and pictures.
Walking tools	going for a walk with a participant to see what they see or hear what they have to say informally.
World views	a set of beliefs about the role of research. Different research philosophies have different paradigms. Also called a world view.

About the authors

Kaz Stuart (she/her) is a social researcher and leader, focusing on socially just methods, creative methods and community enquiry in research. She strives to create more equity in society through research, theory and practice. Kaz has achieved this through varying roles throughout her career, including as Director of Strategy and Learning at The Centre for Youth Impact, as Honorary Professor and as Director of the Centre for Research in Health and Society at the University of Cumbria.

Lucy Maynard (she/her) is a social researcher working with people, communities and organisations in social innovation and impact. As a practice-based researcher, Lucy strives to create more meaningful, embedded and equitable approaches to participatory research, evaluation and impact measurement. She has achieved this through her work as Principal at The Australian Centre for Social Innovation, as Director of Projects at The Centre for Youth Impact, as Head of Research at Brathay Trust and as a visiting research fellow at the University of Cumbria.

Acknowledgements

Our thanks go to the research groups who have contributed to the shape, content and style of this book:

- Ewanrigg Girls Gang
- Preston Community Foundation Researchers
- Blackpool Headstart Resilience Revolution Researchers
- The National Youth Agency Youth Researchers Network
- Carlisle Youth Zone Young Researchers
- William Howard School Young Researchers

In writing this book we hoped to achieve a rich blend of theory and practice – enabling practitioners, groups and communities to engage in participatory research in practice that is informed by theory. Reflecting this, we have two forewords, one from a practice perspective and the second from a theoretical perspective. Thanks to Deborah and Lonnie for their kind support.

Foreword

Deborah Terras
Principal Youthwork Specialist at
The National Youth Agency

As a Youth and Community practitioner, I firmly believe participatory research underpins the core youth work principles and values as well as supporting the four cornerstones of youthwork, those being education, empowerment, equality and participation. This book, and the work of Kaz Stuart and Lucy Maynard, has opened up an accessible world for those who traditionally may not have seen a role for themselves and their communities within participatory research. It is an invaluable toolkit for practitioners, young people and communities to use. Kaz and Lucy guide you through the world of participatory practice, unpicking and explaining the academic language, offering a 'real life' grounded approach to research. The book provides a clear and accessible step-by-step journey for the reader. It uses examples about real people and communities who have developed and led research, generating a collaboration of stories that can be shared while recognising and acknowledging the value of the knowledge generated.

I really wish this book had been part of my researcher journey when I first entered the world of academia; it is an invaluable resource for everyone to use and is well placed to break down the barriers of accessibility to participatory research and, in turn, promote action for change.

Foreword

Lonnie Rowell
Co-founder & Founding Chair, Action Research Network
of the Americas (ARNA), President, Social Publishers
Foundation (SPF), Co-editor, Educational Action
Research (EARJ)

This is a small book with a big heart. Determined to avoid writing an overly academic book, Kaz Stuart and Lucy Maynard have created a practical book for people working in community-based settings who want to examine the strengths and weaknesses of their practices and take steps to improve. The big heart in the book is how clearly and strongly Stuart and Maynard embrace the potential of participatory research to empower both practitioners in local community settings and the community members that practitioners serve. This embrace is not easy to maintain, and the determination to see it through can be enhanced through the use of this book.

Readers, practitioners of participatory action research and advocates of engaged and responsible civic life will find this book a worthy companion. The book has a clear aim: 'to help organisations and practitioners across a wide range of fields to do research with the people they work with'. Stuart and Maynard firmly believe more research in practice is needed to better understand and develop practice from within organisations and within communities. They recognise that the way research is done should be guided by the people the research matters to, 'rather than being externally "done to" them'. Their approach to participatory research, with its emphasis on working with both practitioners and community members to engage them as much as possible in the research, reflects a larger social movement to democratise knowledge production and dissemination.

The authors make their case in the book's introduction for grounding their work in knowledge democracy. Knowledge democracy is a phrase that refers to long-standing conflicts over what constitutes knowledge, how it is created and whose knowledge counts. The phrase has been advanced as a kind of platform for resistance to the domination of long-standing and privileged academic platforms that have too often tended to colonise the production of knowledge. Knowledge democracy seeks to break the grip of this colonisation and its faulty assumptions about people and their lives.

Participatory research as presented in this book serves knowledge democratisation both through the recognition evident throughout its pages that participatory research is conducted 'closer to the ground' with the intention of solving practical problems and enhancing practices to benefit local populations. In these respects, participatory research has great potential to reinvigorate a democratic spirit of seeking solutions to real world problems in communities. As the writer, educator, conservationist and activist Terry Tempest Williams puts it, 'when minds close, democracy begins to close. Fear creeps in; silence overtakes speech'. To the extent that participatory research demonstrates its practical and localised intent, there is a greater chance of opening dialogue and lessening fear. As Tempest Williams further puts it, 'democracy is best practiced through its construction, not its completion'. With a greater emphasis on the democratic construction of knowledge, perhaps we can better open spaces for community-based conversations that link research to a more participatory orientation within local communities and neighbourhoods. Overall, Stuart and Maynard have produced a book that reflects the recognition that the often-rarified air of advanced scientific understanding disseminated through elitist knowledge platforms has to be put in balance with the capacity and determination of regular folks to understand their situations and to take appropriate actions to improve things. Their book illustrates how participatory research, conducted in a collaborative manner with humility and determination, has a chance to contribute significantly to the opening of speech, the nurturance of democracy and the fostering of creative solutions in relation to the crisis-ridden times we live in.

Written in a practitioner-friendly voice, the book includes excellent examples and tools from the authors' varied and deep involvements with community-based initiatives in diverse settings. The book is organised and written to be an easily accessible resource, with an inviting and supportive tone throughout. Efforts to encourage and practice participatory research are crucial to challenging the impact of the anti-democratic movements found around the world. When done responsibly and diligently, which is just what Stuart and Maynard are advocating and providing the tools for in their book, knowledge democratisation helps bring the lived experiences of average citizens, as well as those often found living at the margins of society, into relevant and central positions in demonstrating how community groups and community members working together can become powerful sources for identifying solutions to community problems.

Introduction

Welcome to the book!

We hope you enjoy reading and using this book. It is written with a clear aim – to help organisations and practitioners across a wide range of fields to do research with the people and communities they work with. We absolutely believe we need more research in practice to better understand and develop practice from within. Practitioners are in a great position to do this. We call this approach participatory research as we work with people and engage them to participate as fully as possible in research.

In order to help organisations and practitioners in their participatory research we have written this book in down to earth, accessible and practice-based language. We know that research isn't many people's day job and often isn't a priority. So this practice-based approach is different to most research books, mainly because it is really pragmatic, based within the realities of everyday practice (limited time, resource, access, buy-in and constant pressure to meet the needs of the people and communities we are working with). At points we have also highlighted common research terms, as some people might be interested in knowing more about what is underpinning this research approach. The book walks you through every step of the research journey as practically as possible, with examples and tools signposted along the way. You could use it as a guide to take the first step in exploring a particular user need that has come to light, or that thing you had always wanted to know more about, or you may have some funding to do some investigation or evaluation of a project. You may read it for interest, inspiration or confidence. You could share it with your colleague, team member or manager to inspire others to think – hey, what if we could just do some research on our practice!

We believe participatory research is a very powerful form of research for three reasons. Firstly, it creates knowledge from people's first-hand experiences (or lived experience), making sure the research, and the knowledge that comes from it, is relevant. Secondly, it ensures the way we do research and the tools we use are guided by the people it matters to, rather than being externally 'done to' them. This means the way knowledge is created works better for the people involved, making sure it is fit for purpose and increases engagement and meaningfulness. Thirdly, taking part in research can be highly empowering, leading people to feel they have more control over their lives – in other words it aligns with social justice. Overall, the outcomes and the process of participatory research can be embedded within our practice and lead to more positive change in our communities for the benefit of the people who live there.

This belief comes from our personal experiences. We have worked together for over ten years carrying out research in practice with fellow practitioners, participants, students, organisations and communities. We are committed to participatory research with people in a wide range of communities and groups and are delighted to share our experiences with you. True to our participatory values, the contents of this book have been co-designed with different groups of community researchers who were keen to share the key barriers and enablers to make participatory research more accessible to others, as noted in the acknowledgements.

We both remember feeling daunted by the ridiculously long words that seem to be used in research, the wide range of choices and the worry that we would get something wrong. Since then, we have worked with many practitioners and students who hold these same feelings. We are determined to break down the barriers and bust some myths that exist between academia and practice and come together to learn from each other's expertise. Our first research book (Stuart, Maynard and Rouncefield, 2015) was written in a more academic style and delves into research more deeply. Whilst feedback was positive we want to go further and reach more people in practice:

> 'It is inspiring and enables me to access the world of evaluation and understand our work in a different way – I'm really excited about the possibilities and feel my practice developing as a result'.

The Practitioner Guide to Participatory Research with Groups and Communities is written from a social science perspective but is interdisciplinary (for example, health care, social worker, community artist) and multi-method (including digital learning, accelerated through the COVID-19 pandemic). We also draw from practice-based examples from across the globe.

We aim to guide you through the complexity of participatory research in a straightforward way. We will walk you through the stages and choices to be made, signposting the safety of participants at all points. You may find it useful to share the book, or parts of it, with the people you are doing the research with. A key principle of participatory research is that we need to support the people we are working with to understand the choices they are making too. Whilst the book is not a toolkit for community members, you can use sections with them to help them make sense of the research too.

How can I use this book?

Feel free to read the book however you like – there are no rules! Read from the start to the end, dip in and out, only use the chapters that sound good – whatever you like!

The book is practically laid out in the order research planning usually follows, starting with the foundational ideas and working through to the fine details. Research, however, does not always follow this 'logical' order. We sometimes start with micro details (for example, three years of survey data that has just landed in our lap) and then work outwards from that. Sometimes we have a group of co-researchers before anything else. Don't worry if your participatory research does not follow this neat and tidy order. You can read each chapter for information, or you can work through the chapters with a real piece of research, using them to help you make each decision. Here is a list of the chapters and what they discuss, to help you find your way around.

We have written the text in a flowing narrative style for ease of reading without extensive references. If you want to read more about the ideas we present in each chapter please visit the further reading which includes a range of electronic resources, papers and books for you to explore.

Chapter 1: Just what is participatory research?
>   This chapter will set the scene by explaining what participatory research is and isn't, and when and why it is useful.

Chapter 2: How do we begin to plan our participatory research project?
>   This chapter introduces you to the steps of participatory research design and how they relate to one another. Even if you do not start your project at the 'beginning' it is useful to see all the different pieces and how they fit together to support each other.

Chapter 3: What do we want to explore and why?
>   This is the first practical chapter which will explain how you go about defining the purpose of your participatory research and the questions that you might want to ask.

Chapter 4: What ideas are the foundations of our research?

This chapter will help you think about some of the values, beliefs and assumptions that will underpin your research and how to keep everything in alignment.

Chapter 5: How will we go about exploring our questions?

There are lots of different ways of doing research which come from different values and beliefs. This chapter takes you on a tour of some of the main ways of doing research and supports you to identify what will work for your project.

Chapter 6: Who can get involved to explore our questions?

This chapter will help you to work out decisions on who might take part in your research, how many of them and how to engage them.

Chapter 7: How shall we collect our data?

There is a wide range of ways to collect research data and this chapter will introduce you to a good selection. The chapter will guide you to choose the right one for your participatory project, or to invent your own if one doesn't already exist!

Chapter 8: What do we do with our data?

This is the bit where some people get confused, worried or bored. But fear not, data analysis needn't be that way. This chapter guides you through some of the key ways to do analysis and particularly how to do this with people in a participatory style to develop a clear set of messages.

Chapter 9: How do we get our messages out there?

Working out what to say is only one part of the challenge. This chapter guides you to think through who you want to listen to your messages, what they will be most likely to pay attention to and how to get this in front of them.

Chapter 10: How do we keep everyone safe?

Safety is always of great importance, and in research projects that process involves thinking through a set of research 'ethics' and working with those principles in mind. This chapter guides you through the most common and gives you some examples.

Chapter 11: Doing and reviewing participatory research

Being involved in research can be a powerful experience. This chapter will support you to review the process of being together doing the research, the work you created through the research and the impact that had in the world. A great opportunity to review regularly and celebrate.

Some quirky parts of the book

We've written the book from a range of different professional or practice perspectives so that it is relatable to as many people, organisations and communities as possible. We've added lots of examples to bring it to life – you may want to add your own examples if ours are not close enough to your community of practice.

There are lots of practical activities that you can choose to do yourself, with the co-researchers or not at all – it is entirely up to you and your learning style! These are signposted as chapter activities or reflective tasks and tea breaks.

Each chapter has a summary and further reading section. These might help you develop your plans, learn more or quickly reconnect with a chapter you read earlier. We hope they help make the book an easy-access resource. There is also a glossary of research terms, for those that want to keep tabs on those long words. The first time we introduce these words we will highlight them in bold so you know you can find them in the glossary.

Finally, we will keep referring to 'cups of tea' throughout the book. All kinds of tea – herbal, chai, breakfast. We have assumed that everyone understands the concept of making tea, even if you don't drink it (ironically Lucy doesn't drink tea and much prefers coffee!). As well as finding that regular 'tea' breaks help research along, we keep referring to them here to anchor all the different steps of research to one very practical thing that most of us do every day – making a hot drink. We hope you find the examples, and the breaks, help you through the book.

Introductory reflective task and tea break

- Why did you want to read this book?
- What are you hoping to gain from it?
- What strategy will you use for reading it?
- Who do you want to share your learning with?

1

Just what is participatory research?

Chapter overview

This chapter will introduce you to what research is generally, before specifically introducing participatory research to you. The benefits and challenges of participatory research will be outlined with reference to social justice. This chapter will help you to understand and in turn communicate to others why this type of research is so important.

Just what is research?

We have a very straightforward and broad definition of research – it is any activity that is focused on exploring a question or questions. There are many different questions we could ask about the world and equally many different types of research to explore these questions. All are useful but choosing the right one can sometimes make research seem very complicated.

As research is about exploring questions, all research will have a **research purpose** – something it is trying to achieve – and one or more **research questions**. Exploring these questions will help you achieve your purpose. All research has a **research approach** – a way of doing something – as well as an output and end product. In this respect, it is a little like making a cup of tea. At the beginning you intend to make a drink (your purpose), you consider what type of tea you want (questions), you have a set of ingredients, decisions and instructions (your approach) and you end up with a nice cup of tea to drink (your **research output**). Just as there are many types of tea and ways to make tea, so there are different types of research and ways to go about it. No single tea or way of making tea is right or wrong, but you might serve the wrong type of tea to the wrong people – with milk when they normally take it without! In a similar way, no single type of research is 'wrong', but you could use the 'wrong' type of research for the questions you are trying to answer.

And what about the participants? You might think that all research needs to involve people, but in its widest sense, research can also include objects, animals, microbes and existing data, and so may not have any participants at all. However, if you are reading this book, you are most likely going to be working with people and so we focus on those types of research throughout the book.

You may have noticed our definition here focuses on exploring questions and not answering questions. This is deliberate because research doesn't always lead to answers! In some instances, it leads to more questions and the exploration continues. Some research does lead to answers, but not always, and so for this reason we just focus on the exploration and having an output.

Key types of research

We like to think of the different types of research as the branches of a tree. We start with the trunk of the tree – all research. At the top of the trunk the tree separates into two large branches. One of these is about proving things – called '**positivist**' **research** as the people who do it want to prove a theory is positively right or wrong. The other branch is about exploring and understanding things rather than saying something is right or wrong. We call this **'post-positivist' research** as it grew after (or post) the positive branch.

The proof (positivist) branch is broadly characterised by testing or running experiments so that you can definitely say that A led to B. Measurement and numeric data is central to this type of research, as well as the idea that the researcher is objective and has no influence on the research.

In contrast, the 'exploring' (post-positivist) branch is broadly characterised by open questions and rich varied perspectives. What people say – word-based data – is typically central to this type of research, as well as the idea that the researcher is subjective and will have an effect on or in the research. The different branches of research are shown in Figure 1.1 below.

At this point of the book, we follow the post-positivist branch as we are interested in a wide range of things that happen in the world, why they happen, how they happen and what that means. A 'yes' or 'no' is not very helpful in answering those types of questions but is brilliant for testing medicines!

The 'exploring' branch divides into multiple different branches, with more growing every day. Each branch is a type of research. We won't go into all of these branches in this book, but we will

Figure 1.1: The research tree

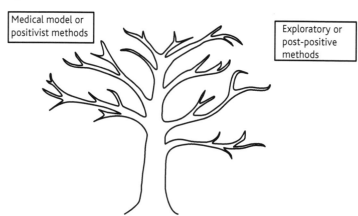

Medical model or positivist methods

Exploratory or post-positive methods

signpost some of the main branches in Table 1.1, so you have a sense of the breadth of exploratory (post–positivist) research and where **participatory research** fits in.

Table 1.1: Types of research

Broad description	Aims to …	Types of research (not exhaustive)
Action orientated	Focus on creating learning and change through and during research	Action research Participatory action research Appreciative enquiry Practitioner research
Evidence orientated	Show how good something is or describe what something is like	Case study Evaluation Comparative studies
Involves others	Support people who are affected by issues to do their own research	Participatory research Community-based research Indigenous research
Culturally orientated	Identify the key features of a culture, group or situation	Ethnography Auto ethnography Phenomenology Hermeneutic research Indigenous research
Creative orientation	Carry out research in creative ways	Visual research Performance research Narrative research Arts-based research
'Power' orientated	Identify the way power affects society	Feminist research Critical research Socially just research
Unobtrusive orientation	Collect data as normally or naturally as possible	Naturalistic research
Open orientation	Develop meaning from what people say rather than from ideas the researchers might have	Grounded theory
Hybrid research	Use a range of methods which are all of value in answering the question	Mixed-method research
Commercial orientation	Find out what people will buy/use and why	Market research User research

None of these types of research are better or worse than another, some are just more suited to some research questions more than others. Although you might think you have this problem solved because you are doing participatory research, you will have to support the group or community you are working with to choose which type of research they want to use to do their research. This is where things get exciting! Whilst participatory research is most certainly post-positivistic, participants could choose quantitative tools (such as a survey that produces numerical data), which stems from positivism. Therefore, you need to be aware of the whole tree and where the different branches meet. There are plenty of online resources to support you to learn about positivist types of research.

It is worth noting at this point that researchers have different ideas about things (have you ever experienced someone putting milk in peppermint tea – very unexpected!). Therefore, not everyone will agree with how we present research in this book, and that is okay. We encourage you to come up with your own ways of thinking about research.

The importance of participatory research

Given there are so many types or approaches to research, why are we focused on participatory research? Let's return to the cup of tea. Participatory tea making, and participatory research, is about the person who is going to drink the tea choosing what kind of tea they want to drink, what they want to drink it out of and how they want it made. Another approach would be to just make the tea for them without involving them (or planning a research project without involving people), but this risks the tea (or research) being the wrong type, presented in the wrong way and/or tasting horrible.

The starting place of participatory research is a little more complicated than other forms of research. We simplify this into three possible scenarios:

1. You may go to members of a group or community wanting to do some research with them;
2. Members of a group or community may come to you wanting you to do some research with them;

3. You may decide together that you want to do some research as you are engaged with other activities with the group or community.

Therefore, if we extend our tea metaphor further, in participatory tea drinking, the group may instigate, you may instigate or you may all decide together to have a cup of tea. However, following this you'll collectively be figuring out how you'll make it.

Banks and Brydon-Miller (2018: 3) provide an excellent definition of participatory research as:

> a collaborative effort in which people whose lives are affected by the issues being researched are partners in designing, undertaking and disseminating research to influence socially just change. The process aims to be democratic, participatory, empowering and educational.

We like this definition as it says who is involved, what they do and how they benefit. Participatory research is about research 'with' people, not 'on' people, and there are many reasons for this. A lot of research used to be done by 'experts' who, very generally speaking, were white, well educated, privileged males from the Western hemisphere. Of course, that is a huge sweeping statement which is becoming less true every day. However, many faulty conclusions were drawn by researchers who did not understand the people they were doing research on. Arguably these people are not best placed to research circumstances, situations, people and cultures that are very different to their own. So, the first reason for participatory research is that the people whose issues need researching should be the people to do (or at very least be involved in shaping) the research, as they understand their worlds best of all. For this reason, we refer to **co-researchers** throughout this book. Co-researchers are different from research **participants** in that they make research decisions with you, whereas participants 'just' provide data in research projects led by researchers. As a research team, you as the participatory researcher and the co-researchers may identify other participants to take part in the research and to explore the research questions. And just to add a layer of complexity, you and the co-researchers may also be participants as you ask each other research questions.

The second reason for participatory research is that groups and communities have insider knowledge about which questions need to be asked and how to best explore them. As experts in their own lives, groups and communities therefore need to be involved in planning and doing the research too. An outside researcher may never be able to fully understand or appreciate a context or community that is not their own.

Researching in this participatory way hopefully means better questions, approaches and understandings, all of which benefit everyone in society. It also means that the knowledge from research is created by everybody rather than just certain types of people, which is fairer. Participatory research therefore has an aim of making knowledge more equitable by deliberately encouraging people who might not usually do research to be involved.

Participatory research also has benefits for the co-researchers. Planning, doing and writing up your own research project can be empowering. It can help communities and groups to feel more in control of their own lives and more able to shape what happens around them. In this respect, participatory research can be disruptive. Groups and communities might become more aware of their own situation, they might be dissatisfied with what they see and might want to do something about it. Disruption can be a catalyst for positive change, and so another benefit of participatory research is **social justice**. In order for the world to be equal, some people need more support than others to make the opportunities equitable. Participatory research is equitable itself in giving support to groups and communities to be researchers, and potentially equitable in outcome as those groups and communities may research issues of inequity that affect them. Creating a world that is more **equal** and **equitable** is called social justice. Maguire (2014: 418) defines participatory research in socially just terms as the:

- Development of a critical consciousness of both researcher and participant
- Improvement of the lives of those involved in the research process
- Transformation of fundamental social structures and relationships.

The difficulties of participatory research

Just because participatory research is meaningful and beneficial does not mean it is easy. Far from it. A number of issues arise in any research, and particularly in participatory research.

One key issue is that participants may not have the skills or knowledge to take part in the project and may need training in order to be able to take part as fully as they would like. This does not mean they all need to do a research course; it's about the practitioner–participatory researcher and the group or community working things out together, co-learning, co-designing, co-researching.

If you work with groups and communities, you will be able to draw on everyone's different skills and experiences throughout the project. This means individuals can contribute to the research in different ways and avoids the research process becoming patronising.

Practitioners and organisations are very busy, and equally participants might have busy lives with many responsibilities to carry out. Being attentive to people's interests, skills and availability is both respectful and practical. People may want to be involved at different levels or at different times. Participation can take many formats, and anyone engaging in any of these formats is great; one is not necessarily better than the other. To reflect this point we have drawn the different formats and roles of participation as a scale (rather than more commonly represented as a ladder) in Table 1.2 below.

What is more difficult to reconcile is that the individual group or community members might have very different ideas of what to research or how to research it. Time together discussing ideas,

Table 1.2: Different formats for participation

One: a person giving data as a participant in research	Two: co-researchers designing the research process	Three: co-researchers conducting the research	Four: co-researchers analysing the research	Five: co-researchers creating the research output	Six: co-researchers communicating the research

working out criteria for which idea to take forward or voting might be necessary to resolve some of these issues. This simple point starts to shed light on the range of skills needed to facilitate participatory research with groups and communities.

It can also be difficult to convince stakeholders (for example, a funder or commissioner) that participatory research is appropriate. That is often because you may not be able to tell them exactly what the research will be on, how it will be done, when it will be done or what the final output will look like. You can't define some elements, as the group or community need to. This is often a limitation on participatory research projects getting up and running. It does not fit well into the tightly defined and scheduled world around us.

Whilst participatory research is about involving people and shifting power from 'academics' to 'communities', it is impossible to get rid of all forms of power. Job title, gender, race and accent might all crowd into the research group, and so participatory researchers need to always be on alert for who has a voice and why, and who is left out and why. This is explored further in Chapter 10.

With all those considerations laid out, we must conclude that it is challenging for practitioners and organisations to undertake participatory research. It is, however, a deeply rewarding and meaningful type of research with power to improve people's lives. We have never regretted a participatory project despite the stresses and strains along the way. We hope this book encourages you along and helps answer the many questions you must have by now.

Tricky terminology

Participatory research has developed many different shapes and forms over its history, which can sometimes add to the confusion we might feel reading about it. Participatory research includes:

- Participatory action research
- Community-based research
- User-led research
- Participatory rural appraisal
- Participatory organisational research

- Citizen science
- Participatory arts-based research
- Participatory evaluation
- Critical pedagogy
- Rights-based research.

If you do some internet searching for 'examples of …' each one, you will get a feel for their similarity in their aim to enable people to participate as fully as possible, and their differences in terms of the ways in which they do that.

Reflective task and tea break one

- Write your own definition of participatory research that would make sense to colleagues or to people in your group or community.

Summary

Research is about the exploration of questions. All research has a purpose, research questions, approach and output. There are many different types of research and this book focuses on participatory research. We focus on this type of research as it supports people in groups and communities to find out about things that are important to them and to become knowledge creators themselves. This grounded and lived experience, we feel, is much needed as the basis for decision making in the world, contributing to it being a fairer and more socially just place. However, there are challenges in doing participatory research, and this book hopes to guide you through these to make your project as successful as possible.

Further reading and resources
- A great overview of all different types of research is a book written by Zina O'Leary: O'Leary, Z. (2017) *The Essential Guide to Doing Your Research Project*, London: SAGE.
- A website with examples of qualitative research in the UK can be found here: https://www.qual.org.uk/qual-practice
- A good guide to participatory research is a book written by Jo Aldridge: Aldridge, J. (2016) *Participatory Research*, Bristol: Policy Press.
- Some examples of various kinds of participatory research can be found here:
  - https://colouringinculture.org/blog/the-morris-justice-project-south-bronx/
  - https://www.youtube.com/watch?v=nm-xSvUKZ_A
  - https://www.youtube.com/watch?v=Jo9RiXpVjYQ
  - https://www.youtube.com/watch?v=meBlI3x0hs0

2

How do we begin to plan our participatory research project?

Chapter overview

Now we know what research is, we can start to think about what it involves and how we plan it. Just as work with people, groups and communities is rarely straightforward, similarly research can have the same uncertainties to challenge us. Therefore, it can be helpful to have a clear and logical set of stages to support you and the co-researchers to plan the research. These can act as check points that can help to guide you in your research journey. Thinking all these steps through before you start, or referring back to them along the way, can help to make the project go as smoothly as possible, just like making a good cup of tea.

Figure 2.1: Let's make a cup of tea!

Let's start with a cup of tea!

When you make a cup of tea you know there are certain things that you will need, and you know they need to be put together in a certain order – for example boiling the water before putting it onto the tea. But there are also lots of choices involved in making a cup of tea too – what sort of tea? Will it need milk and sugar? What should it be served in? Those are design choices, and it might depend on what the situation is and who you are with as to which type of tea is appropriate. Designing research is similar in that there are a range of stages that usually happen in a set order and each involves a lot of choices, but once you have the hang of it, it comes naturally.

So **research design** involves thinking through the steps in planning your research.

The stages of research design

We are going to introduce ten broad stages in a research cycle as shown in the diagram below (Figure 2.2).

Each of these stages is discussed in a chapter of this book. If you follow the stages in the diagram they will help guide you through the research project. Whilst we plan research in a step by step, or linear, approach, you will probably find you have to keep moving backwards and forwards across the steps as a decision made in one step will affect the decisions in another. It is completely normal to zigzag back and forth through the steps. As each chapter of the book tackles each stage of research, you can easily revisit a key topic or problem by dipping into the relevant chapter. We also found that one enquiry often leads to another, so you might find yourself leaping from number ten back to number one with a new question.

Figure 2.2: The ten steps of research design

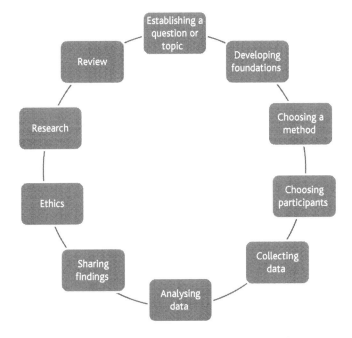

A short overview of each stage is provided below to help you to see the whole picture and to navigate from one step to another.

Deciding on your purpose, aims and questions

You would be amazed how often people set off on a research project without really knowing why they are doing what they are doing. Knowing your 'why' is helpful to come back to if (or more likely when) you get bogged down in some of the details to follow. This is your bottom line, your back stop, your point! It could be that you really need to know more about x before you can do y; you want more information on people's opinions of xx; or it just all comes back to xxx. There are some big questions for you and the co-researchers to answer in this chapter, such as why we are doing this research, who will it benefit, what we hope it will achieve. These will help you work out the **research purpose**, what you hope to achieve by doing it (the **research aims**) and what you specifically want to know (the **research questions**). These are your foundations, so it's worth spending time on getting them as solid as possible. This step can also involve reading around the subject to work out what is already known about the topic you want to research and how it is viewed by other stakeholders such as the government, media and other researchers, communities or organisations.

Identifying your core beliefs

We all have core beliefs about the world which we rarely put into words. We might all, for example, believe that the world is round and that we won't 'fall off it' if we travel to another continent, but we never say so. There are some important patterns and sets of beliefs that influence the way in which we go about research – they are our foundations from which we can build. There is some complex language surrounding this, such as 'research paradigms', but we use the term **research philosophy**. Whilst these are slightly different, we think more practitioners will relate to the word philosophy and so we are sticking with that! For example, some people think that we can prove that everything is either 'right' or 'wrong'. This is one common pattern of belief or philosophy that researchers have. We will unpack the other patterns that might apply to you in this chapter. Understanding and stating your (you and the co-researchers) beliefs is important as it influences how you do your research, what tools you use and how you analyse your data. This in turn will then influence what sort of information or '**data**' you collect. To keep things straight forward, we'll focus on three main types of data – number data, word data and visual data. These types of data fit into different patterns of beliefs and so identifying your core beliefs will also help you decide which of these three, or which combination of these three types of data, you will use.

Working out how to go about the research

Once you have your foundations in place, the logical next step is to consider how you 'do' the research with your co-researchers. We call this the **research approach** and it includes the methods you use – a bit like the 'method' part of a cookery recipe; it maps out how you go about the research. There are many options here, and this chapter gives you an outline of each and how to decide between them. Some of your choices will be directed by your core beliefs, but you will still have options no matter what your foundations are. If you believe black tea to be the most refreshing you may, for example, reach for a kettle at this point. However, if you believe iced tea to be the best, you may be reaching for some ice. Both types of tea are delicious and may be refreshing to different people, and the choice between them will dictate very different methods in the kitchen.

Working out who and what will be involved in answering your questions

Now you know what you are going to research and how you will do it, you are able to think about where or who you and the co-researchers get data from. You may start by thinking of the best places or people to get this information from, who will know the most about it or whose ideas and beliefs are important to include. Often, but not always, this involves **research participants**, but sometimes can involve other sources, such as observations or archived sources of information. You will start to consider things such as how many participants you need, who they will be, what characteristics or demographics they will have. Practical decisions now kick in as you work out where these people are, how you can get information and an invite to them and how you can best engage them.

Working out how to collect each bit of data: data collection tools

Surprisingly this is often where people start research design. Many people say 'let's interview someone' or 'let's use a self-esteem survey' before really thinking through what they are doing and why. Deciding on the **data collection tools** before anything else can lead to all sorts of issues and so we recommend thinking through the earlier chapters first, but if you haven't – no big deal. A data collection tool is just a short way of saying the way you will get the information.

By now you hopefully have a good sense of what you want to know, how you will find it out and who from. This next step is about putting the details in place. You will decide how to best collect each bit of information or data. The decisions here must match up with the method you decided on and the people you have decided to work with. There is a wide range of tools to choose from and you will get an overview of these and handy tips on how to decide between them.

This step also involves planning the practical details of who's doing what, when and where. Knowing these details is important so you are all clear.

Working out what the data says

Working out what the data is telling you is called **data analysis**. There are some practical step-by-step ways to make sure you get the full meaning out of the data you have collected. This is the step that people most often leave out of their planning altogether, waiting until they are sitting in front of a pile of data before they consider how to tackle it. So, taking time to plan now really helps. This will involve thinking through which type of analysis fits your underpinning ideas and data.

Planning what to tell who and how

Although you have not got your findings at the planning stage, you should have some sort of idea of what you might want to say and who you might want to listen to what you have got to say. This step involves planning how to best get your message across to those people and how to do it. Research can turn up surprising things, so you may need to adapt your communication plans as you go along, but you should have a plan in place before you start researching. The jargon for this area is planning your **research dissemination strategy**, but 'communication plan' works just as well!

Making sure everyone stays safe

Of course, we want everyone to stay safe whilst we do research! This process is called planning the **research ethics**. This step will ask you to consider how people's identities are kept safe, how the data is managed so it is secure, what the benefits are to people taking part, how to check they understand what is being asked of them and so on. We plan research ethics in advance of the research to ensure everything we have in mind is appropriate. It may be that having thought through the ethics you may want to go back and revise some of your other plans.

Ethics don't stop at the planning stage either, sometimes ethical issues crop up whilst we are doing the research even though we tried hard to avoid them. We have often learned the hard way and will give you some top tips from our experiences for managing ethics in the moment.

Doing the research

This is the bit you have all been waiting for! You have patiently and diligently planned the research following all the steps and are now ready to go live and get on with your project. This step is where you think through how you will do things, in what order and who will do each task – that will help you get everything done well according to your research design. You will walk back through each step but in a practical way delivering everything you and the co-researchers have planned – good luck!

Reviewing the research

Good research involves reviewing throughout as well as at the end – reflecting on what you are all doing/have done in order to work out how well it all went and to learn from the process. Plan this now! If you don't agree on how, when and where you will review, it is likely you will forget it in the rush to get on with the next part, the next research project or certainly the day job! Take the time to celebrate your achievements, to identify what you have learned and how you can put that into practice.

Exploring the match between stages

You may have gathered that we think the matching up of decisions from one step to another is important. Some people set out to understand how much tea people drink in a day by asking them to take a picture of their brew because they think photo data is an original and engaging approach. This approach might be best to work out what strength people like their tea, or what cups or mugs they like to drink it from. But, unless you asked people to take a photo of every cup of tea, you would not get the number data you were looking for. Some people like how simple numbers seem and so ask people to rate how much they enjoy tea on a 1–10 scale. Whilst this might give them a rating it does not give them any information on why they enjoy it, where or with whom, which would be important in an exploratory study.

Ensuring a good match between each stage therefore makes sure we get the information we want in a way which suits the co-researchers so we can tell the story we need to the people who need to hear it. It prevents us from doing our 'favourites', picking and choosing what we like rather than what is appropriate, and leads to high-quality research which can contribute to change.

Reflective task and tea break two

Write down your answers to these questions:

- How would you describe each of the ten stages to the co-researchers?
- Can you say why each stage of research is important?
- How much time will it take you to plan each of these before you start your research?
- How can you ensure everyone in your team will be up for working through the design steps?
- Where can you go if you get stuck on any of these stages – what or who could answer your questions?

Summary

This chapter has given you a map to navigate your way through research. The map has been broken down into a series of small and achievable steps to support you to design a high-quality research project to embark upon. Planning and then conducting these one at a time gives you a starting place, even if things emerge in a different way and you need to adapt. The following chapters will give you more detail on each. You have also started to learn some of the research 'language' in this chapter. Researchers seem to have particularly long and complicated words to say what they mean. Sometimes these words are useful shortcuts saving you a lot of explanation, but they can also be very off-putting and can stop other people understanding them. We use everyday language and research language in this book and it is up to you which you choose to use when you talk and write about your research – which to use will depend on who the co-researchers and participants are and who the audience is. This book will hopefully help guide you through the participatory research process so that you can guide your communities and organisations through it – your choice of language will be a key part of making that a success.

Whilst each step has been described one at a time you might find you need to hop backwards and forwards until your decisions all align. The summary at the end of each chapter will help you work out where to go next. If you are writing a research proposal or a research methodology to go in a report, paper or assignment then you will find each of these steps provides you with a heading and paragraph to write explaining the design choice you have made and why it was the best decision for the research.

Remember there is a glossary at the front of the book with the meanings of all the research terms as a handy guide.

Further reading

- The Association for Research in the Community and Voluntary Sector have an excellent toolkit that works through all of these stages available here: https://arvac.org.uk/resources/
- This website underlines the importance of research design: https://www.reboot.org/2012/02/19/design-resea rch-what-is-it-and-why-do-it/
- This website gives some further guidance on research design: https://www.iedunote.com/research-process

3

What do we want to explore and why?

Chapter overview

This chapter will support you in developing a research aim and research questions for your participatory research project. We will start with an explanation of both and then offer you some tips to develop them for the project with a group, organisation or community. This chapter also introduces the idea of 'locating' your study in a wider field of literature so that you know what other people think about the area you are exploring.

Research aim

At the start of a research project it is useful to have a shared goal you are all working towards. This is called a **research aim**. Your aim will identify what you want to research (the topic or content) and what you want to achieve by doing the research (the benefits). It is really important that time is dedicated to this process, so everyone involved in the research project feels engaged, involved and represented. What and why you do the research is perhaps the most fundamental decision of all.

Equipped with a research aim (and question, as discussed later) you can be clear about the focus of the research and you will be able to explain your research easily to other people. The research question will also help you to have boundaries so you are clear what is included and excluded from your study – this will help you to stay on track.

There are several ways to work out what topic you will research together and how you do it will vary by the context and the people you are working with. Broadly, you will need to explore all the different topics that the co-researchers might be interested in. Interests might come from things the group have experienced themselves, things they have noticed around them, things they have read or heard about in the **media** or things that are important to the communities they live or work in. All of these sources for inspiration are equally valuable.

Developing a list of topics is most commonly achieved by talking together in a group and drawing a **concept map** of all the possible topics. For each idea put forward, the group discusses the second question – why it is of interest and what are the benefits of doing it? This helps in developing the idea further. Some discussion of how the research might be approached and who the participants might be may also emerge at this stage. At the end of these discussions your group will have a well-developed list of possible projects. We've seen some interesting developments of this stage where some groups have used storyboards, images or an illustrator to draw out the ideas so everyone can visualise what has been suggested. Other creative tools such as this will help bring various ideas to life and make the experience more engaging and meaningful.

We will assume you will use your own group work and facilitation skills in selecting which idea or ideas you choose. If you use a voting or scoring system however, it might be important to point out areas such as cost, ease of delivery or impact in the community. How you decide on a research topic must also fit well with the cultural norms of the people you are co-researching with.

Once you have decided on your topic and the benefits of the research you can turn that into a single sentence which will be your research aim. Here is a handy guide to writing an aim:

- Start with 'This research aims to ...'
- Add a verb to show what you want to do as a team (examples could include: test, prove, explore, map, understand, reveal, illustrate, demonstrate, describe, identify ... many other possibilities!)
- Add the topic (for example, climate change, relationships, COVID-19 ... millions of possibilities)
- Narrow the scope as much as possible to a specific context (for example, climate change in 2020 in the Southern hemisphere).

For example, the aims of one of our recent projects reads as follows:

> This research aims to explore the benefits of participatory research for 35 young people in the north of England.

There is no 'right' or 'wrong' when developing a research purpose. The most important thing in participatory research is that it engages everyone who is part of the research process. Hundreds of purposes are possible for every topic – find the one that resonates the most with everyone.

Returning to our example of the 'cup of tea', research aims could include:

... to understand the importance of tea ceremonies in different countries
... to explore the physiological effects of drinking tea in 18–30-year-olds
... to map cultural differences in tea drinking globally
... to test the effect of altitude on stewing tea.

Chapter activity

Have a go at developing a research aim for a project you have delivered in the past, are delivering currently or hope to deliver in the future.

We've developed criteria to help ensure your research aim is as good as it can be. With the aim you wrote above, you might like to check through the following questions:

- Is it interesting to everyone in your group?
- Will it be interesting to anyone in the wider community or society?
- Is it focused and specific with a narrow and clear topic?
- Does it develop new knowledge or a new way of generating knowledge?
- Will it create possibilities for positive change?
- Is it possible to do this research? Can you gather the information you want to?
- Is it manageable? Is it too big for your team or timeframe or resources?
- Does it clearly show the topic?
- Does it say what it aims to achieve?

You may want to revise the research aim if it doesn't meet these criteria. When you evaluate your research, either throughout or at the end of the research process, you can revisit this aim and decide, as a group, to what extent you achieved it.

Research questions

A research question is simply a question that a research project sets out to explore. You may be able to have one research question, or you may find you need a few. Try to have as few as possible in order to keep the research manageable. The research question/s should link directly to the aim and use the same words but posed as a question/s rather than a statement.

A thorough group discussion is needed again to develop your research question/s. One way to do this would be to write the research aim in the centre of a piece of paper, whiteboard or computer screen, and then ask everyone to develop questions about that particular topic based on what they might want to gain more knowledge on. As with the research aim, you will then need to narrow down on a few which are of the most interest or significance to the group. The research questions will help you keep focused and will ensure your efforts in the research are all useful.

Research questions will start with a questioning or interrogative word. In English, the most obvious examples include; what, which, when, where, who, why and how. You need to develop a question for each of the parts of the research aim that you think are important.

To return to one of our research aims – 'This research aims to explore the benefits of participatory research for 35 young people in the north of England' – we have the following three research questions starting with what, who and which:

- *What are the benefits of participatory research reported by young people?*
- *Who benefits from each of these – do they vary by age, gender, socio-economic status?*
- *Which research design features enabled young people to gain these benefits?*

Chapter activity

Have a go at developing some research questions for a project you have done, are doing, or hope to do soon:

1.
2.
3.
4.

At the end of the research you will revisit your research question/s as a group and decide to what extent you answered them.

Here are some criteria for assessing whether you have designed a good research question:

- Is the question important to the group?
- Does the question sentence focus on only one thing rather than several?

- Is the question specific, defining what the focus is?
- Is the question clear, avoiding vague words such as 'some', 'a few', etcetera?
- Will the answer to the question be more than a 'yes' or 'no'?
- Is the question concise and easy to understand?
- Is the question doable with the resources you have?

Re-visit the questions you have just written and see if they could be developed.

Contributing to social justice through question design

Participatory research is an approach to social justice itself in that its key principle (participation) supports people who would not usually be involved in research design to generate knowledge themselves in ways that are meaningful to them, about topics which are also important to them. This stands in contrast to research traditionally designed by academics and done 'on' or 'to' people, on topics that primarily interest the researchers. Enabling more people to generate knowledge is called a **knowledge democracy**; producing knowledge in more democratic ways. So the very act of asking a group, community or organisation to define the questions that are important to them is a step towards knowledge democracy and social justice itself.

There is also the possibility that the research topic will be an aspect of social justice too. A 'socially just' question would be concerned with any groups that are particularly powerful or powerless, the reasons for those positions and the very different outcomes they create. Socially just research concerns itself with inequality and inequity in any shape or form. Your participatory research does not have to tackle a socially just question, but it is an excellent opportunity to be socially just and contribute to positive change.

Locating your study in wider literature

Locating your study means reading around a little to work out how your views and findings sit amongst the other voices on this topic. This might show that your research purpose is in line with or affirms what other people are saying. You may also find that your perspective is entirely new and different to what everyone else is thinking. That is your research position – you are then located either alongside or away from the other voices. Another word used in research for these other voices is '**discourses**'.

The view of the government is possibly one of the most important voices to understand your positioning with or against. This is important as it will enable you to see how controversial your research might be. In some countries it is safe to do any research into any topic. However, in some countries it is not safe to be researching something that does not align with government views. This step is therefore an important safety check for your group before you go any further.

The government's view is most visible in three ways. The first is the legal system in your country. The government will have passed **laws** to make people do things in certain ways. Check whether your research is legal itself and whether it challenges any laws in your country. The second form of government view is in their **policies**. These are the published documents which state what must be done and guide how things are done nationally. You could check whether there are any policies that relate to your research topic. Finally, members of government sometimes speak in public and sometimes do so more freely than they would in a document. **Speeches** are also, therefore, a good place to find what the government's voice is.

The media is also an important 'voice' on your topic because it is so influential. What the media says can shape how society thinks. The media includes newspapers, television broadcasts and online news outlets. These might be tightly controlled by and therefore aligned with the government, or there might be a wide variety of media voices spanning the political spectrum. It will be important to see what the media says about your research topic.

Other **research literature** is another key voice in the background to your study. It is useful to find out what other studies have been conducted, how they did their research and what they found out. Again, this will allow you to see if your research fits into this existing body of work or is new and different. This isn't always situated within academia; it could come from other research in practice like your research.

The fourth 'voice' comes from **theoretical literature.** These are written by people who think and write about a topic without necessarily doing any research themselves. Theoretical literature can be written in academic papers or books and give you a sense of how other people think about your topic.

You may find a lot of other material out there which relates to your topic but isn't from the government, media, researchers or theorists. Because of the uncertain status of this other 'stuff', we call it **grey literature**. This often includes reports by organisations or opinion pieces. You can use these if they are particularly relevant or present an important view on your topic.

Now we know about the different types of voices (or discourses), we can turn to the practicalities of how to find them and record them. There are three steps here: working out what literature you will include, searching for and storing the literature and reading and writing it up.

What to include

There are hundreds of pieces of information you could use and you don't want to get lost in them, so keeping a tight literature search strategy will be really important. You may not have much time or resources for this activity, so you will need to keep it as narrow and tightly controlled as possible.

Consider:

- What topic words will you search for (for example, tea consumption, tea growing, tea ceremonies)?
- What date range will you use (for example, 2020–22)?
- Which country of origin will you draw from (for example, China only)?

Finding the literature

There is a wide range of ways to find literature on your topic, sometimes called a **literature review** of **literature search strategy**. You could start with community resources – what does everyone in the group know of and have access to already? You could have a session where everyone brings in something (a book, a newspaper cutting, something they heard) and map it on the wall, poster or online project board. Using the internet is a very obvious place to look – you may not have access to fancy electronic databases of literature but there is an amazing amount of literature anyway. A simple search for your topic keywords should produce lots of results which then need to be scanned through to filter for the most appropriate ones. A good strategy is to search for the type of literature and your topic name, so for example, using the criteria on the previous page:

Tea production statistics 2020–22
Tea production policy 2020–22
Tea production media stories 2020–22
Tea production research papers 2020–22

If you are struggling to find research studies on your topic, you could use a specialist search engine such as Google Scholar to refine your search and to get rid of some of the grey studies.

Trusting the literature

It is important to trust the source and content of your literature. In academia, searching is easier as there is a clear hierarchy. However, this is harder when including the other sources we describe here. For each source you will need to work out how trustworthy it is or whether the authors have some hidden agenda.

Recording and sharing the literature

You need to decide what you will do with all the research you acquire so that it is a resource for the whole research group. You could save everything you find in an electronic folder that everyone can access. But that makes assumptions about everyone having access to the internet and being digitally skilled. It might be more beneficial to print everything out and keep a research folder. Again, there are assumptions here about everyone being able to read. An audio recording or folder of pictures might be more useful. You will need to talk with your co-researchers and find a way to store and record everything in a way that is accessible to everyone. This goes beyond the literature and refers to every part of your research project.

Reading and writing it up

This step could be done by one or two people who like reading, or each person in the group could take a section of literature to review. You will need to discuss the best way to go about it with the group. Rather than reading everything from front to back you need to skim read the documents as they can be very long.

Here are some tips for skim reading if it is new to you and your group:

1. Read the title – does it relate to your topic? If not, discard it.
2. Read the abstract or executive summary – research papers and reports often have a summary or abstract at the start. Look for key messages that relate to your topic. If there are none, discard it. If there are some, highlight them or write them down (paper, wall chart, notebook, online project board, spreadsheet).
3. Read the contents – are there any sections which are relevant to your research topic? If so, highlight or note down which ones. If not, discard it.
4. Related contents – go to the section or chapter which seems to relate to your topic. Read the title, summary, headings and conclusion to see if you can get what you need from those. If there is anything of particular interest, read that section in full.

You are looking for short clear statements about your topic which you can use to show that person's or organisation's view. Whether you are working online, in a notebook, on index cards or on a wall chart, you want to develop something like the below for each of the four types of literature.

Climate change and tea production statistics 2020–22

Statista Tea Worldwide presents these highlights:

• Revenue in the tea segment amounts to US$232,381.2m in 2021. The market is expected to grow annually by 8.20% (CAGR 2021–2025).
• In global comparison, most revenue is generated in China (US$92,397m in 2021).

• In relation to total population figures, per person revenues of US$30.92 are generated in 2021.

(see https://www.statista.com/outlook/cmo/hot-drinks/tea/worldwide). You are only looking for the very key points rather than long statements and paragraphs or you will end up with too much. Bullet points are usually helpful. You also need to note down where you got the information from (for example, the report name and authors). Skim reading and summarising is a skill which you may need to support your group members to develop.

Once you have skimmed a few relevant pieces of information from each type of voice or discourse, you can start to write about the context, or a **context statement**. As well as stating what the other relevant voices say, you also need to state how they relate to or influence your research. This would be a paragraph or two on each type of voice along the lines of:

> The statistics on the impact of climate change on tea production is ... this paves the way for / this is a barrier to this research / this challenges the views of this research team. ...
>
> The media presents the impact of climate change on tea production in a range of ways. X, for example, states... whilst Y says ... This research is more aligned to X than Y in that.

This context statement, informed by your literature review, helps the reader understand how your project fits in with everything else said on the topic. It will be a particularly important section if you are applying for funding as all research funders require a statement like this.

We have talked about you doing a literature review here to inform your context statement, and, just to add confusion, literature reviews are also a form of data collection and could appear again in step five (Chapter 7). When used as a data collection tool, the process is the same but includes many studies and is much more detailed in style. If you want to understand what is known about a topic then it could be a tool to choose, but otherwise this short and simple review will work just fine.

It is also worth saying that not all research includes a literature review, however we have supported groups through this process and they found it a valuable, if challenging, part of the research and a really helpful life skill, so please do include it if you can.

Reflective task and tea break three

Consider your answers to these questions:

- How can you make sure the selection of a research aim and the research questions are as inclusive as possible?
- Who might get left out of the decision-making process and why?
- How can you make a decision in a way that values everyone's opinions?
- To what extent will a literature review be valuable to the study and the co-researchers?

Summary

This chapter has introduced you to the idea of a research aim and research questions and has given you a structure to write your own. We've given you some guiding criteria so you can judge the quality of your research aim and questions. We also discussed the ways in which the research process is socially just and explained that your research aims and questions may or may not be socially just too. The chapter then explained how to locate your research amongst other voices on the topic and gave you some tips on keeping control of the mass of literature you could use.

Further reading

- This small book walks you through the process of designing research questions: O'Leary, Z. (2019) *Quick Little Fixes: Designing a Research Question*, London: Sage.
- This YouTube clip is also a good guide to developing research questions: https://www.youtube.com/watch?v=1oJNO6PYZe4
- This video explains social justice in simple terms: https://www.youtube.com/watch?v=O5uKJVDFHFw
- And this video explores social justice in more detail: https://www.youtube.com/watch?v=Wtroop739uU
- This website is a useful tool for developing skim reading skills: https://www.bbc.co.uk/teach/skillswise/skimming-and-scanning/zd39f4j

4

What ideas are the foundations of our research?

Chapter overview

This chapter will explain some of the core beliefs associated with different types of research. This is important so you know what underpins your research and so you can identify what might be informing other people's thinking. This is about understanding different perspectives rather than working out a 'right' or 'wrong' approach. The chapter will give an overview of **research philosophies** and then dig into some key ones more deeply before supporting you to work out which philosophy is forming the foundations of your research project.

Research philosophy

The way we approach research is based upon certain beliefs and assumptions about the world, what there is to know in the world and how we come to know it. These beliefs act as a guiding principle for our behaviour or how we construct and conduct research. This is also referred to as our research philosophy. There is often discussion within this of the nature of 'existence', 'reality' and 'truth'. We are not going to discuss these here, as we want to keep things straightforward, but feel free to explore this further – perhaps starting with our other book (Stuart, Maynard and Rouncefield, 2015).

These underpinning ideas are complex and change over time, so let's look at a real-world example. The most common starting place is how people once believed the world was flat. This was because people believed they should trust what they saw and that reality was what could be seen. From this, knowledge and truth were constructed first hand. This philosophy of first-hand observation had served people very well and was a reliable way of going about life. Only then did we discover the world was not flat, it was found to be round, and so the belief that you should believe what you see was challenged and a new philosophy of testing ideas was born. The old philosophy is not wrong – if I see a cup of tea in front of me, I believe it is there for me to drink. But another philosophy is also true – that I will only really know if the tea is there if I try to pick it up and drink it. Therefore, all philosophies can be true at the same time. This is why we keep saying there are few things that are absolutely right or wrong in research, but some things may be a better fit than others.

You might now be wondering how many different philosophies there are and what they are called. This chapter will introduce you to a range of research philosophies, but it is important to note here that philosophy is a huge field developing over hundreds of years (think Aristotle!) and so there are many different views of it. This is particularly the case in research where different authors and researchers argue about different words and concepts. This can seem confusing when read in different places. What follows is our view of research philosophy and we hope it is helpful, but it is by no means definitive.

So let's try and keep things straightforward. We can understand our underpinning philosophy by asking ourselves some simple questions:

- What do we want to know, why do we want to know it (**our aims, purpose, and questions**)?
- What do we think is important and what do we value about this; what are our core beliefs about truth and knowledge; where can this come from and who has this knowledge (**our philosophy**)?
- How do we go about knowing it, exploring it, analysing it and sharing it (**our approach**)?

A participatory philosophy

The research you are doing with a group or community is participatory – hence you reading this book. Therefore, we will start by defining the participatory philosophy before moving on to other types of research philosophy.

The bedrock

The fundamental belief underpinning participatory research is that research itself is a political act and power should be distributed to everyone. What that means is that research findings are often used as the basis or justification for economic and political decisions that affect everyone – in this respect it is political in its output. Secondly, research has traditionally been conducted by privileged people (to grossly over-generalise: white, male, upper class) – a political elite. Participatory research therefore believes that more people should be involved in designing and conducting research, generating their own findings to influence the world. Thirdly, the way in which research has been conducted has mostly fitted with a Western medical model of 'truth' using tests and numbers to generate knowledge. Participatory research is grounded in a belief that knowledge can be generated through different types of research methods that are more inclusive than tests alone. Finally, the results of participatory research are thought to have benefits to those involved – increasing their sense of empowerment – and also benefits to society as it disrupts power dynamics and shapes the world on the basis of different knowledge. Participatory research is therefore thought to have the potential to be transformative. These beliefs – sharing power, inclusion, a breadth of methods and transformation – shape the way participatory research is done.

Foundation one

For participatory researchers, there is no single definition of 'the truth' in terms of human experiences. Rather, a wide range of truths exist at the same time. We may all like or dislike tea, for example, and we are all 'right' in those views although they are different. Different versions of the truth will vary through time, culture, social setting and personal experience. Therefore, participatory researchers seek to design research based on different people's experiences and knowledge. It throws out the assumption that 'researchers' know best (know the truth about research design) and instead asks groups and communities what questions are worth exploring, who should ask the questions, how it should be done and what should be done with the findings. Individuals, groups and communities' 'truths' are just as important as the researcher's. Equally, the findings from the research conducted by individuals, groups and communities is just as important as that conducted by researchers; perhaps more so.

Foundation two

As participatory research values different versions of truth, then accessing those different forms of truth is dependent on people collaborating. Co-researching with people in groups and communities is therefore the cornerstone of participatory research; it is how knowledge is generated. In order to enable everyone to participate in research a second factor becomes important here – accessibility. Long words, formal settings (such as universities) and formal relationships may be barriers to engagement and involvement. Participatory research is fundamentally concerned with making research accessible, engaging and meaningful to people.

Foundation three

Participatory research is socially just in its commitment to sharing power, transformation, the privilege of different perspectives, importance of co-research and commitment to inclusion and accessibility. Participatory research does not just believe everyone should have equal opportunity to participate in research (for example, responding to an online survey), but that a wide range of people should be able to access additional support and opportunity to design, conduct and participate in research; it is committed to equitable research opportunities.

The way these foundations become reality is evident through the time the research takes and its relational approach, in the depth of trust and collaborations and in the respectful engagement and involvement of groups and communities in research and its design. The foundations are also evident in the ways the co-researcher's knowledge, experience and skills are valued, and the ways in which they are supported to gain whatever additional research knowledge and skills they need. They are also characterised by an adherence to the design choices of the group in terms of purpose, aims, philosophy, method, analysis and dissemination. These foundations are shown in Figure 4.1. Participatory research on a cup of tea might ask:

Figure 4.1: The foundations of participatory research

Foundation 1: There is no single truth in lived experience	Foundation 2: Research should be accessible and inclusive	Foundation 3: More support is given to people less involved in research

Participatory research is a political act

So, we are interested in researching tea:

- Why are we all interested in it?
- What do we want to find out about tea?
- Why do we want to find that out?
- How do we think we could go about this?

Other types of research philosophies

In Chapter 1 we introduced you to the research tree with two different branches of research. These are grounded in different research philosophies. They are like different places on a spectrum rather than opposites. The different research philosophies represent all the different places across that spectrum, or all the different branches on the tree.

Whilst the research you are doing with a group is participatory, it may be that they want to do research that comes from a different philosophical position, and that is why we explain the different types here.

Positivism, or 'scientism' or the 'medical model', of research is about proving things are right or wrong. The beliefs of this approach centre on reducing the variables so something is clear and validating theories or hypotheses. This philosophy believes that reality is objective, provable and constant. For example, a cup of tea is always a cup of tea. From this perspective, truth and knowledge are generated from tests and experiments and so research practices feature observation and measurement (such as testing the temperature of the tea).

At the other end of the research spectrum or tree is post-positivism. This came after positivism (hence the 'post') and is very different. This philosophy believes the world is a complex and dynamic place that needs exploration in order to understand it. Post-positivists believe the nature of reality is subjective – that means it is different to different people, and therefore incredibly varied. This perspective might take the temperature of the tea above and seek to understand more subjectively what temperature different people prefer to drink their tea. Further, a cup of tea is very different in different cultures, countries and contexts and to people with different tastes. There are hundreds of realities of 'a cup of tea' depending on who you are and where you are. At home 'tea' might be a social occasion of interaction, whilst on a mountain it might be a life-saving drink.

There are several shades of post-positivism which are presented in Table 4.1, each subtly different. For example, **interpretivism** focuses on how different people interpret the world. Building knowledge is therefore grounded in conversations with different people in order to understand their different perspectives, and it would be unlikely to arrive at a single simple answer, whilst **constructivism** really emphasises the importance of individual experiences, meaning making and beliefs. People's characteristics, context and history are thought to influence the way they construct reality. Therefore, reality is thought to be subjective and varied, whilst knowledge and truth is constructed by people through their conversations and daily actions. As such, open ended and exploratory methods are needed to understand how people have constructed those meanings. This might mean talking to different people about what a cup of tea means to them in order to understand the range of meanings it can have in people's lives.

The participatory philosophy (as you will know by now) believes that research is a political act which has been dominated by the powerful for too long. As a result of this belief, it seeks to build a new 'reality' and to understand the current reality through the work of different people in society. Engaging people to collaborate in research is therefore key to building knowledge and truth and participatory methods are used. This philosophy is considered to be the most socially just as it seeks to re-distribute the power of research and knowledge generation and to build a better world from the views of more people.

In the middle of the research philosophy spectrum, or tree branches, is **pragmatism**. This philosophy focuses on practical, real-world solutions. Reality is viewed as constructed by people and therefore variable, but also as something that is observable and measurable. From this perspective a cup of tea means different things to different people and can be made in hundreds of ways, but it is still a hot drink in a container that people consume. Its reality is both changeable and fixed. This reality is therefore

Table 4.1: Types of research philosophies

Research philosophy	Core beliefs	Beliefs about the truth	Beliefs about how knowledge is made	Research approach (practices/ behaviours)
Positivist 'Scientism' Medical model	Determination Reduction Validating theories	Objective Things can be proved to be right or wrong	Built through tests and experimentation	Observation and measurement Quantitative methods
Post-positivist Pragmatism	Real-world solutions are needed Practicality	Reality is the consequence of real-world actions It is fixed and variable at the same time	Built through measurement and exploration	Measurement and exploratory Qualitative and quantitative methods
Post-positivist Interpretivism	Exploration Understanding Complexity	Subjective Variable	Built through conversation, expression and exploration	Open-ended, explorative and creative Qualitative methods
Post-positivist Constructivism	Individual experiences and beliefs matter	'Reality' is constructed by people socially and over time (historically) It is subjective and multiple	Knowledge and truth varies by person and so is only ever partial It is constructed and discovered	Exploratory Qualitative methods
Post-positivist Participatory research	Research is a political act and power should be distributed to everyone	'Reality' should be built and understood by different people	Knowledge must be created by different people in collaboration	Collaboration Involvement Whatever methods the group want to use

explored through measurement and exploration in order to build both types of knowledge about it, and so relates to a mixed-methods approach.

Research approach

Research approach is discussed in the next chapter, but it is important to point out some key principles here as we ask ourselves some of the philosophical questions that framed this chapter. Our philosophy leads us to an approach and to particular methods we will use to gather the type of data that we value, as indicated within Table 4.1.

Across the research spectrum, or branches, there is a preference for different types of data. Positivist research seeks **quantitative data** that provides numeric measures and proof which matches its philosophy. In contrast, at the other end of the spectrum, post-positivist philosophies seek **qualitative data**. This suits the exploration of human thoughts, beliefs, experiences and perspectives. Qualitative data includes verbal or written words, images, pictures, movement, sounds. As you may have guessed, pragmatic and mixed-method research seeks both qualitative and quantitative data so that it can quantify and qualify research responses.

Let's discuss this with a cup of tea! In fact, think of a community 'tea morning' for older adults over the age of 65.

One group wants to adopt **quantitative methods** because they want a definite and numerical answer to the usage of a community tea morning for over 65-year-olds. They want to know how many, how often and how long people stay at a community tea morning. They want to be as objective as possible and quantify how important this time is in order to get more funding for more community tea mornings and believe having numerical data will be the most powerful way to convince funders. Therefore, they use quantitative methods which will impact the sample of participants, the data collection tools, the way they analyse the data and the way they present findings.

A second group wants to use **qualitative methods** because they want to understand the needs of over 65s at the community tea mornings to establish if and how a community tea morning meets their needs. They want to be subjective and qualify what, in particular, people need and how best to meet this need and they believe this will come from a deeper and richer understanding of people's experiences in order to improve practice and provision, as well as convince funders. Therefore, they use qualitative methods which will impact the sample of participants, the data collection tools, the way they analyse the data and the way they present findings.

A third group wants to use **mixed methods** (including both quantitative and qualitative methods) as they want to both quantify – through numerical data – and qualify – through rich insights – in order to have a more holistic understanding of the over 65s' community needs. They want to have an objective and subjective view and believe only using one approach would not give a full and rounded understanding and this is really important in proving and improving community provision and evidencing this need to funders. Therefore, they use mixed methods which will impact the sample of participants, the data collection tools, the way they analyse the data and the way they present findings.

Research alignment

Research alignment ensures all the research design choices are lined up. Think of a tower of children's building blocks: the more closely they are aligned the stronger the tower will be. The same is true of the research. We need all the different parts, or stages, of the research process to be aligned to make the research as robust as possible. Figure 4.2 illustrates this point – if these are out of alignment, the tower will topple over.

Earlier in the book we said that there are no right or wrong decisions in research; it's all about making the best decision for your particular research question and population. Whilst we're sticking to that claim, the place where research might go most 'wrong' would be in a misalignment of the steps of research. Here's an example to understand this a bit better.

Imagine your research question is 'what is the chemical compound of green tea?'. That is a positivist question with a simple answer in the form of a chemical formula. It would therefore be misaligned to go about that with a constructivist study, asking every third person you meet on the street what they think. You don't want to know what people think about it, you want a scientific proof of the formula. Similarly, if you wanted to

Figure 4.2: Research alignment

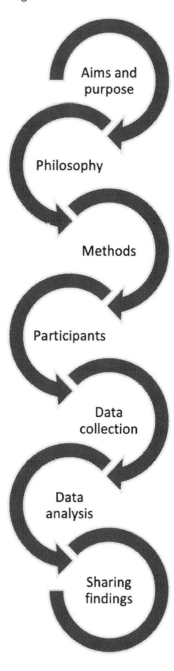

know 'what meaning does tea hold in people's lives?', it would be misaligned to do a scientific study. You could test the tea all day long, but scientific tests would not provide you with people's perceptions. A participatory, constructivist or pragmatist study would be better aligned.

How much do you share?

This discussion of philosophy is on two levels – the first, as detailed above, being to establish the socially just values of participatory research, and the second to understand different philosophies in order to support different perspectives within the group of co-researchers. If we think a little further about the second of these two, we need to understand that different group members may have different belief systems from within the Table 4.1 and thus may value different approaches to and ways of conducting research. You may end up supporting many of these as a participatory researcher. Engaging with co-researchers involves collectively deciding what type of research to conduct. Your knowledge of different philosophies will help you guide the co-researchers in collective decision making and alignment, starting with the questions we discussed earlier in this chapter:

• Why are you interested in the topic?
• What do you want to find out about it?
• Why do you want to find that out?
• How do you think we should do that?
• What do you think we could do with the findings?

You are likely to be facilitating the decisions the group is making and their access to supporting knowledge from differing philosophies. How much of the underpinning philosophy the group wants or needs will vary, but you can be prepared to guide them with the basics we have set out within this chapter. We do not think people need to be research experts in order to do research, but we do think having some knowledge can empower and liberate people doing participatory research.

Reflective task and tea break four

Write your reactions to these questions:

- To what extent might your personal views affect your research philosophy?
- Is it possible to be 'unbiased' or 'neutral' as a researcher?
- How might it feel to do research within an approach or paradigm that you do not agree with?

Summary

This chapter has provided an overview of research philosophies, how they are constructed and how they vary. The idea of research alignment has been introduced to help you to work out which philosophy is appropriate and what that means for your research. We have also suggested that your role, in facilitating or leading the participatory research, is to support co-researchers in understanding their research philosophy, depending on how much they want and need to know.

Further reading

- This book gives a detailed but quite technical account of the history and theoretical roots of participatory research: Shubotz, D. (2020) *Participatory Research: Why and How to Involve People in Research*, Sage: London.
- Whilst wider than the field of research Pete Beresford's book gives an excellent overview of participatory philosophy and ideology: Beresford, P. (2021) *Participatory Ideology from Exclusion to Involvement*, Bristol: Policy Press.
- Whilst detailed, some excellent guides to the philosophy and practices of working from a non-Western perspective can be found in these invaluable books: Archibald, J., Xiiem, Q., Lee-Morgan, J. and De Santolo, J. (2019) *Decolonising Research – Indigenous Storywork as Methodology*, London: Zed Books.
- Patel, L. (2015) *Decolonising Educational Research*, London: Routledge.
- Tuhiwai Smith, L. (2012) *Decolonising Methodologies* (2nd edition), London: Zed Books.
- Michelle Fine's book is also an excellent dive into socially just research: Fine, M. (2018) *Just Research in Contentious Times*, New York: Teachers College Press.
- This YouTube clip gives a good overview of a paradigm, ontology and epistemology: https://www.youtube.com/watch?v=hkcqGU7l_zU
- This gives a good overview of the research philosophy of participatory research (called ideology in this website): https://www.participatorymethods.org/task/research-and-analyse

- This useful guide also locates participatory research as a paradigm – you might like their clear explanation of it: http://communitylearningpartnership.org/wp-content/uploads/2017/01/PARtoolkit.pdf
- You might also like to read this example of community-based participatory research: https://bmcpublichealth.biomedcentral.com/articles/10.1186/1471-2458-13-91

5

How will we go about exploring our questions?

Chapter overview

We have defined our purpose and aims, set out research questions and identified our underpinning research philosophy. Now we are going to focus on the next level of detail – how we approach the research. This takes us from the more abstract and philosophical ideas into a more practical discussion of how we 'do' research. This chapter will explain what research methods are and give an overview of participatory methods. We'll then go on to provide a summary of the rest of the considerations within the research approach before the subsequent chapters tackle each of these parts in turn, guiding you through the choices you may need to make with the co-researchers. We will introduce three case studies within this chapter – adding more applied research experiences to abstract tea drinking. These are fictional case studies to emphasise key ideas. They are constructed through our own experiences and the experiences of other participatory researchers.

Aligning our research approach

As we have already discussed, the alignment between all the research steps is crucial and particularly so here, moving from philosophy to approach. If there is a misalignment then the final research is unlikely to meet its purpose and aims.

Our research approach consists of several smaller building blocks. These steps are considerations in the research approach, making the process you follow clear and ensuring you have a plan – this is especially important when working with co-researchers. The steps are:

- The methods you'll approach the research with – we described these broadly in the previous chapter as qualitative, quantitative and mixed methods.
- The sample or research participants – who you and the co-researchers will involve in the research; how you will recruit them; what will engage them.
- The data collection tools – the specific ways in which you will collect data, for example interviews or surveys.
- Data analysis – the ways in which you will analyse the data you have collected to generate findings.
- Research ethics – the ways in which you plan to keep everyone safe in the research.
- Quality measures – how you plan to ensure the research is of good quality.
- The dissemination strategy – how you will share and communicate your research findings to the wider world.

Participatory methods

In the previous chapter, we described qualitative, quantitative and mixed methods and the difference between them based on what their underpinning philosophies valued. We also stated that a participatory approach prioritises collaboration and whatever methods the co-researchers choose. Therefore, they may choose quantitative or qualitative, or mixed methods.

OK, enough of the tea! It's time to get real and bring this to life a little more. Through the rest of the sections of this chapter, and in all subsequent chapters, we are going to work with the following three case studies:

Group A is a group of young people from a school in the UK. The participatory researcher approached them to see if they wanted to explore the increasing need for mental health provision in schools. The group wanted to have as objective a view as possible on this and adopted quantitative methods to explore mental health provision as they believed the statistics they saw within the media were powerful and influential and they want numerical data to relate to this.

Group B is a group of parents from a large city in the USA. They approached the participatory researchers to support them in exploring their concerns about police stop and search amongst the children and young people within their community. They wanted to have a subjective view on this and adopted qualitative methods to explore people's experiences of this within their communities as they believe this is complicated and nuanced and people's lived experience is powerful and important to share.

Group C is a group of multi-agency practitioners working in community development projects across India. They came together on a leadership development training programme and wanted to explore common experiences in engaging their teams in multi-agency working. They wanted to view this both objectively and subjectively and adopted mixed methods to get a rounded understanding of the problem.

Each of these methods may lead to different people participating in different ways within the research. The people who participate are called the **sample** and we will discuss these next.

Participatory sampling: an overview

As you may have gathered by now, 'sampling' is about working out who might engage in the research. First we will look at sampling at the co-researcher level and then from the perspective of having established a group of co-researchers, who then want to work out who they could engage as research participants. In Chapter 1 we defined three starting points of participatory research:

1. You go to members of a group or community wanting to do some research with them;
2. members of a group or community come to you wanting to do some research with them; and
3. you decide to do some research together as you are engaged in other activities with the group or community.

In some instances the group is self-selecting and in others you are more likely to be looking to find people who are either, or all, of the following to be involved in the project (as in starting point one):

a. Not usually included in research;
b. have skills, knowledge, experience that will be beneficial to the research;
c. would benefit from the process of co-researching; and
d. want to be involved in research.

Let us now look at sampling from the perspective of having established a group of co-researchers who want to work out who they could engage as research participants. If your research was exploring 'the mental health benefits of tea drinking for ageing people across the world', you would be likely to only include people who drank tea and should include groups of people from around the world. The possible sample is enormous, so you might need to reduce it with some other logical decisions – perhaps people over 65 who drink tea more than three times a day in each capital city in the world. This is likely to still be too large, but you hopefully get the principle that you are trying to create some 'rules' to identify who would or would not be able to participate.

Types of participation

As a reminder, in Chapter 1 we talked about different types of participation and stressed that these are not necessarily 'better' or 'worse' than one another, but rather different options will be suited to different people and situations to different extents. Participatory research is a move away from doing research 'about' groups of people as the object of a research study and towards people doing research about their contexts themselves.

Framing this with co-researchers is an important step in order to understand that there are different types of participation that could be equally necessary. Jo Aldridge (2016) presents a model in her book on participatory research, which could be a helpful framework for co-researchers' understanding. For Jo, there are four positions of participation within research, some more passive or active than others. These are shown in Table 5.1.

We would say this is also about levels of choice. The very lowest level of choice being at the left-hand end, with, for example, consent to use anonymised personal data to understand trends, that is the participant is passive as an object of the research. Choice increases as the participant chooses to engage in research as a subject of the research and increases further as they may choose to act in the research, for example they choose how they want to share their lived experience. Choice is at its highest at the right-hand end, and participants may want to become part of the co-researcher group.

The degrees of participation in Table 5.1 will be important for you and the co-researchers to understand the different positions as you decide who the sample of participants may be.

As participatory research has a commitment to include people who may usually be excluded, working out how to access

Table 5.1: Degrees of participation

Degree of passivity	Passive	Active		Social change
Participant position	Participant as object of the study	Participant as subject of the study	Participant as an actor in the study	Participant co-designed or led
Outcome	Tokenistic from the perspective of the participant	Recognition of the participant	Inclusion of the participant	Emancipation and empowerment for the participant

Source: Adapted from Aldridge (2016: 156)

them and how to work with them safely might be problematic. Particularly younger or older participants or people with learning disabilities might need additional support. People with a range of transitory or migrant status might be difficult to work with practically as they change location frequently. People in some life circumstances may need some additional support to be involved.

Considerations for each of these groups are dealt with in more detail in Chapter 10 on research ethics. However, it is important to point out here that we reject definitions of such people as 'vulnerable' or 'at risk' as we feel these terms disempower and stigmatise people who have a range of skills and abilities. Rather we see people living in certain situations or as having certain experiences. In this way we seek to have an asset-balanced approach acknowledging both needs and strengths. We further reject definitions of these populations as 'hard to reach', with connotations that they are deliberately elusive or evasive. We believe definitions should shift to the researcher not being able to engage them. We prefer to advocate for creative approaches to engagement and additional support.

Let's return to our case studies:

Group A was a group of young people from a school in the UK. They wanted to adopt quantitative methods to explore mental health provision. As such, they wanted to get as large a sample of students as they could from their whole school to relate their data to national statistics. Therefore, their sample selection ensured the participants were active in the study. They chose this, rather than looking at school data on numbers of mental-health-related absences – which would have been more passive.

Group B was a group of parents from a large city in the United States. They wanted to adopt qualitative methods to explore parents' experiences of their children being stopped and searched within their communities. They wanted to share their own experiences with each other as they knew there was a lot to gain from sharing their own powerful lived experiences that others could relate to. Therefore, their sample was themselves, and they were the actors in the study.

Group C was a group of multi-agency practitioners working in community development projects across India. They wanted to adopt mixed methods to get a rounded understanding of engaging their teams in multi-agency working. Therefore, their sample included their team members.

Engagement and recruitment

The next stage of the sampling process is working out how to engage and recruit people into the research. This involves thinking through how to best communicate with them, what messages to convey and how to make joining the research a practical possibility for them.

There are some interesting nuances within our three case studies that are helpful to draw out here.

The group of students wanted to work with large numbers from the whole school. They choose to promote this by putting up posters and speaking in assembly and to each year group. They shared how they wanted to hear everyone's voice and how each of them knew someone who had been affected with issues around mental health.

The group of parents recruited and engaged via Facebook as this is how they already communicated with each other within a support network. There were some parents who engaged in the research and some who did not but still remained active within the original group.

The multi-agency practitioners made time when they came together each month in the leadership training programme to decide recruitment and engagement strategies. They then went back into their individual teams to enact this. They decided to try and do the same thing for consistency and so used an email template promoting the research and a slide deck was used to present at a weekly team meeting.

One of the greatest gifts of co-researching is the co-researchers' ability to engage participants into the research. Their networks and connections afford access to engagement and recruitment in ways that other researchers may never achieve.

Our role as participatory researchers at this point is to support decision making about sampling, recruitment and engagement. For example, for Group A, was a sample of the whole school overly ambitious and what about the differences across this age range? For Group B, was a sample size of just themselves large enough and what if they didn't have time to engage? And for Group C, would there be time to discuss the research at team meetings, which already had a packed agenda? Would a separate meeting be better or risk non-attendance?

Participatory data collection tools

Given that participatory research is about the more active involvement of people in research, it follows that the data collection tools used should enable participation. Usually, the prime question in selecting data collection tools is what will best suit the research questions, but in participatory research the consideration of the needs of the co-researchers and participants is of prime importance.

A balance of practicalities, participant needs and research questions are drawn together when selecting tools. Further considerations need to be made in participatory data collection tools around such areas as literacy, multiple languages, face to face, phone or online – to name but a few.

When considering participatory research with co-researchers the choice of data collection tools is up to them depending on what they want to research and if they engage participants – who they are and their needs. This means you may need to support them to develop experience, knowledge and skills in using different data collection tools. You don't need to be experienced at all of them but work with them to up-skill in using particular tools.

Let's return to our case studies to see what choices they made about data collection tools.

The group of students wanted to hear the voices of large numbers from the whole school. They chose to survey as many students as possible across all ages as they wanted numerical data and valued quantitative methods. They rejected using an evidence-based inventory to measure student's mental health (as the students would become more of an 'object' of the research), as well as rejecting interviews, as they wouldn't be able to gather larger amounts of data.

The group of parents wanted to explore each other's experiences of their children being stopped and searched within their communities. They chose to interview each other as they wanted rich stories and valued qualitative methods. They rejected using focus groups as they wanted to gather richer, in-depth, personal accounts. They also wanted to support each other on a one-to-one basis and felt learning listening skills through interviewing could really help this longer term.

The group of practitioners wanted to get a rounded understanding of engaging their teams in multi-agency working. They chose an initial short individual survey with both open and closed questions, and individual and team 'value maps' carried out through a team focus group, as they wanted a holistic understanding and valued mixed methods. They rejected individual interviews as they really wanted to be action-orientated and develop their team as well as gather data.

These examples show alignment in the purpose, approach, sample and tools and illustrate that all research designs are 'good' as long as they align and serve the purpose you intended.

Participatory research is open to use a broad range of tools, which is often helpful when working with people who are in complex or challenging life circumstances – as a great deal of participatory research does. There is often a move away from 'traditional' tools (such as evidence-based measurement instruments, surveys and formal interviews) towards dialogical and creative tools. These are grounded in relationships and allow for extended dialogue, ultimately helping rebalance power, which is at the heart of participatory research.

However, there is an important caveat to this in that this all takes a lot of time. More creative data collection tools often take even more time to explore with the co-researchers, as well as then in preparation, delivery and interpretation (data analysis is discussed further below) because the co-researchers are immersed in a process of reflection and creation, and often allow more nuanced and richer data to emerge. Further, whilst surveys and interviews are reliant on language skills, arts-based and creative data collection tools are not, enabling people with different skills to participate. Given that participatory research values different versions of reality from different people and champions inclusion, a range of data collection tools are often used to build a fuller picture of the topic being researched. Flexibility to change tools if they are not working for the participants is also important, placing the needs of the participants over those of the researcher, co-researchers and research plan. This is also a departure from more traditional research.

Participatory data analysis

A range of approaches to analysis exist and it is important (again) to use the right one for the type of data you have collected. Quantitative data, for example, would be analysed with a range of statistical tools, whereas qualitative data can be analysed with a range of interpretive tools. We will discuss these in detail in the data collection tool chapter (Chapter 7).

In participatory research you will be collectively deciding what analytical tool suits the data you are planning to collect and how you will do that as a group. Many participatory research projects fall at this point for a range of reasons including co-researchers becoming daunted or bored by the idea of data analysis, or because the practitioner researcher feels they have to take back control. We have found that data analysis can be easily demystified and happily shared with co-researchers. Using the analogy of building a jigsaw is a helpful way to approach data analysis and we will go into this more in the analysis chapter (Chapter 8). There is also a wide range of creative and digital tools to aid collaborative analysis which we will discuss later too.

Returning to our case studies once more:

The group of students recruited support from their maths teacher at this point who helped them do different levels of statistical analysis on their survey data.

The group of parents recruited someone to transcribe their interview recordings and then went through these with the participatory researcher to draw out key themes together by colour coding the text.

The group of practitioners allocated someone from the group to analyse the survey data descriptively (rather than being concerned about more complicated statistics) and they analysed the value maps collectively within each team and then as a group of co-researchers – drawing out key themes.

Because participatory research involves the researcher and co-researchers in the research, it is important that there is also some analysis of how you as a group could influence the research. This is where reflective or reflexive work can come in. Asking ourselves why we made certain decisions and choices along the way, what it was about us that shaped them and what impact that had will be a useful addition to the analysis of the data collected.

Research ethics for participatory research

Research ethics are a set of principles or commitments to protect research participants and researchers from harm. Working with participants as co-researchers is slightly more complex than in other forms of research. In most other forms of research where participants are objects, subjects or active participants, you will still hold the power as the researcher, deciding what is or is not going to protect everyone involved. When working with co-researchers, you have responsibility for the co-researchers as well as the role of supporting them to have responsibility for each other and any participants they wish to engage.

Additional ethical concerns may also arise when working with people who have additional needs or who live in challenging situations. We'll explore all of these in more detail in the ethics chapter.

Working through a set of key questions in the ethics chapter will help you pre-plan to avoid any ethical issues, but that does not guarantee issues will not also arise and we will share some scenarios with you to think about in-the-moment ethical decision making.

Chapter activity

As a practitioner, we're going to assume you know a lot about keeping people safe. So, let's put it to the test! Think about each of the three case studies we've introduced you to and for each one note down any ethical considerations you can think of to keep everyone (including yourself) safe. We'll discuss these further in the ethics chapter (Chapter 10).

Quality participatory research

Quality research is research that is 'good'. This might seem straightforward, but different standards exist for judging what is and what is not 'good research'. From a positivist perspective, good research has statistical validity and is standardised, large scale and definitive. Those characteristics do not hold true for post-positivist research, such as participatory research. Here, transparency, credibility and authenticity are the hallmarks of good research. Small samples of data are valuable and varied methods and results are all important parts of the research.

When working with co-researchers, deciding what 'good' will look like is part of the sharing of power. As well as how transparent, credible and authentic the research is, the quality of participatory research might also be measured by the extent to which it was participatory, achieved the aims of the participants and contributed to social change. This will also be situated within the philosophical foundations of the method the group chooses.

Let us return to our case studies to exemplify this:

The group of students decided 'good' was defined by the number of survey responses and being able to relate these to national datasets. They developed their understanding of 'good' by including the target of a certain number of responses from all age groups in order to ensure data was as representative of this age range as possible.

The group of parents defined 'good' as supporting people to share their lived experience and feel heard. They asked one another how it felt to tell their stories to one another, and positive responses were used as a sign that the research had been 'good'.

The group of practitioners defined 'good' as teams having greater understanding of their shared values through participating in the process of the research. They valued the change that happened as a result of the research as a sign of its quality.

Disseminating participatory research

Disseminating research is another term for sharing or communicating research. At some point all researchers need to decide who they want to communicate their research findings to, what format that audience will be most attentive to and how to get it to them. That's all part of the communication or dissemination strategy. When working with participants as co-researchers you will be making collective decisions. Rather than the researcher named as sole author, all participants will be named. A range of creative and digital forms of communication might be more appropriate for the participants to create or for the audience to receive, and so the consideration of this is important – research does not always need to lead to a formal report.

In our case studies, the student group's top priority was to influence mental health provision and so they decided they needed a formal report that was comparable to national reports they had seen. The group of parents decided their top priority was presenting lived experiences with powerful narratives that were relatable to not only each other but to influence broader community stakeholders – including the police and policymakers. They recorded short powerful recordings of transcripts, each illuminating different key themes that emerged. The practitioner group wanted to funnel their findings. They produced an interactive infographic showing big-picture themes through to individual examples that brought their findings to life.

Reflective task and tea break five

Consider the components involved in participatory research that we've outlined in this chapter and that are detailed in the framework below. Think

of a group you have worked with or are looking to work with and note who makes the decisions in each row of the framework. We've included the students' case study as an example, as these were important to us when we were looking for a group to work with to explore student mental health.

	Our example: student group	Your example:
Research aims and purpose	Find a group of young people who want to explore mental health provision in schools	
Research questions	Students decide	
Research philosophy	Students decide	
Sampling	Students decide	
Data collection tools	Students decide	
Data analysis	Students decide – where can we get additional support with quantitative data analysis?	
Research ethics	We need to be really careful about supporting any mental health needs that might come from this (co-researchers or participants). Need support/services to signpost to	
Quality measures	Need to make sure students take power, as we are going to them	
Dissemination strategy	Students decide	

Summary

In this chapter we have moved from abstract philosophical foundations of participatory research to how we'll approach doing it. We've explored the different components of the approach when working with co-researchers and introduced three case studies to bring this to life. The following chapters explore each of the components and the different considerations in more detail.

Further reading

- Louise Warwick-Booth and colleagues have written a really helpful book reflecting all the different components of the participatory approach: Warwick-Booth, L., Bagnall, A. and Coan, S. (2021) *Creating Participatory Research. Principles, Practice and Reality*, Bristol: Policy Press.
- This Institute of Development Studies website has some further information on levels of participation: https://www.participa torymethods.org/task/research-and-analyse
- Here is a good explanatory video from McGill University on the power changes involved in participatory research in health: https://www.youtube.com/watch?v=86aoV5uYZgs
- This video is a great example of youth-led participatory research in Kenya: https://www.youtube.com/watch?v=pvsNeKlbbss

6

Who can get involved to explore our questions?

Chapter overview

This chapter will delve a little deeper into who could be involved in participatory research. As we have discussed in previous chapters, there are various starting points for participatory research. Once co-researchers have come together, they then make decisions about who else can be involved, how and in what way. We will discuss people's involvement in terms of target populations, sampling and recruitment strategies.

Who to involve in research

At the heart of participatory research is the assumption that involving diverse people in research design and delivery will make the world a more socially just place. This is based on the belief that a wider range of views of what knowledge is, how knowledge is built and what needs to be known is beneficial. Considering who could be involved in research is therefore of central importance.

As we have already discussed, the group you work with as co-researchers is usually established in one of these three ways:

1. You go to members of a group or community wanting to do some research with them.
2. Members of a group or community come to you wanting to do some research with you.
3. You decide to do some research together as you are engaged in other activities with the group or community.

Let's draw from our three case studies straight away in this chapter to exemplify these three starting points:

In group A, participatory researchers sought out a group of students to explore mental health provision in schools.

In group B, a group of parents approached the participatory researchers to support them in exploring their own experiences of police stop and search of their children – the parents were the participants.

Group C, the group of multi-agency practitioners working in community development projects across India, came together on a leadership development training programme and wanted to explore common experiences of engaging their teams in multi-agency working. The leadership development trainers on the programme became the participatory researchers.

It may be that your participatory project has been initiated by a group of people, in which case the co-researchers are already there. Alternatively, if you are starting a project based on an issue then you will need to consider who will have insight into this issue. This might be the people it most affects, the people who are trying to tackle it already or the people with nothing to do with it at all, but some other form of interest or expertise. As participatory research aims to be inclusive, as wide a range of people as possible would usually be invited, meaning you need to identify and overcome as many barriers to involvement as possible.

The first part of this chapter is going to focus on how you come together as a group of co-researchers, regardless of how you were formed. We'll move on in the second half of the chapter to how you support the co-researchers in the process of recruiting participants to the research, if they choose to do so.

Who are all the stakeholders?

We recommend starting with a stakeholder map – like a **concept map** or mind map of all the people who could be involved. This works well whatever the starting point and will help you to see the range of possibilities and relationships between everyone – including barriers or enablers to involvement. We've found it is then helpful to take all the names we have identified as stakeholders and to place them into a power and influence matrix (see Figure 6.1). This will help you all to understand different people's positions of power.

Figure 6.1: The power and interest matrix

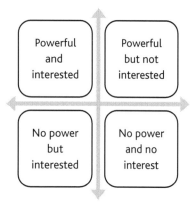

What is power?

This matrix begs the questions – what is power? And why would people be interested in it?

Power comes from a range of sources. The most obvious are perhaps spending power (for example a funder or commissioner) and political power (for example a local authority). People might also have power because of the place they work or their job title. Some sectors of work or roles are considered more important than others. Having responsibility for something is another source of power, perhaps a local community volunteer controls access to a group of people you wish to speak with. Power comes from our personalities, and you may find you add someone to the list who just seems to command everyone's attention or respect for who they are. Power also comes from what people know and who they know and so finding people with personal experience of your research topic and who know others affected or interested by it could be important. Participatory research often places this form of power at the top of the pile, as the most useful basis for generating knowledge. Other more hidden forms of power may arise from gender, ethnicity, age, regionality, accent and other demographic factors. These may need careful attention too.

Let's return to our case studies to explore this.

In group A the participatory researchers were keen to run a student-led project and asked the school as gatekeepers and power holders to allow the project to happen. Once up and running, the students then used their power to invite a maths teacher to help them with their statistical analysis, showing just how much the power had shifted.

In group B, there were obvious tensions and mistrust between the community and the police because of the stop and search context they were investigating. Therefore, there was reluctance to have any police association for fear this would affect engagement and people sharing their stories freely and without fear of reprisal from the police or other community members. However, this was balanced with a desire for the police and policymakers to know they were doing this research as they wanted to share their findings in order to influence policy and practice. The research was designed in a way that participants were protected from the power of the police whilst it happened and yet had the potential to use their power to later influence the police, as you will read in the chapter on dissemination (Chapter 9).

In group C, the group of multi-agency practitioners co-created the project from common experiences shared within the training programme. There was fear amongst the co-researchers that their individual teams and team members may not want to engage because of the nature of the problem – being siloed in their practices, rather than working collectively as local multi-agency teams. Because of their leadership positions, they were also conscious of their power and people in their local teams feeling like they had to participate, creating some particular ethical issues we will explore later in Chapter 10. Equally, this was a team development opportunity that could have immediate positive impact for the teams.

Co-researcher empowerment

It is important to remember involvement in participatory research values empowerment. Involvement could be empowering for someone as they may not have understood their position previously as one of power. However, within the research context they may find they have power as knowledge holders, and thus their position may change on the matrix – from no power to realised power.

We think of empowerment as an ongoing process that starts with awareness (of the research project, of themselves, of the others in the group, of the shared issues), leading to them making choices about the project (what to do, how to do it, who to do it with, what to share) and enacting these choices by actually doing the research (Maynard and Stuart, 2018).

As discussed in Chapter 1, finding the right way to work with co-researchers is a central value in participatory research. Some theorists refer to this as a **cultural competence** – being able to read and match the norms of the people you work with. Participatory research is a highly relational process grounded in open, respectful communication. You will need to communicate through words and actions that everyone is valued and welcome, and that you are all making decisions together rather than running the project yourself. It may feel awkward initially as co-researchers might look to you to make decisions. You are also a knowledge holder and therefore a power holder – you've read this book to start with, giving you some research knowledge and power! Working out how much of that to share with the co-researchers is an authentic and complex process. You do not want to withhold information assuming they cannot manage it nor overwhelm them with too much too soon. Therefore, enabling co-researcher empowerment might be very gradual. Perhaps low-key choices are open to everyone to begin with (refreshments, venue, timing, duration, etc.) whilst you guide the opening stages of the project. Over time, as people's confidence and empowerment grows, they will be able to make decisions for themselves and you might find yourself taking a back seat. In turn, the co-researchers will gain an understanding of their power and role in relation to the research participant's empowerment. Participatory research is distinct from other forms of research in its extension of the traditional 'researcher' role into a complex and dynamic 'research facilitator role'.

Who is interested in getting involved?

There is also a wide range of reasons for stakeholders being interested in the research. Monetary interest might come from people knowing they'll be paid in acknowledgement of their involvement in the project. Political interest could come from people who think involvement will position them well in their community or elective processes. Professional interest may come from sectors who support people with these issues or provide services that are relevant to the project. Community interest could be sparked by the benefits the research might bring to a place or issue. Finally, personal interest could come from experience of the issue or knowing people who experience it.

It's a lot to untangle, but mapping out who has power and interest, and what kind of power and interest, will guide you to think about people's involvement. Having some foundation knowledge and a framework, like the one in Figure 6.1 above, can help you as a participatory researcher in discussions with the group of co-researchers. Discussing why everyone is involved (their interest) and their contribution (power and skills) will be a fantastic starting point showing the value of the whole team. Having tackled their own power and interest issues, the research group will then be well equipped to consider who they invite into their research as participants of the research.

Issues with defining groups

One tension participatory research grapples with is the definition of populations. As a socially just research approach, participatory research aims to describe people in respectful and non-deterministic ways. This ideal is confronted with the reality of societal norms which tend to label groups of people in negative and limiting or 'deterministic' ways. Our preference is to refer to people in terms of the experiences they have or circumstances they find themselves in. Rather than referring to 'gangsters' for example, we would talk about 'people who are gang affected'. There are three reasons for this. Firstly, by referring to the situation rather than the person, we keep open the possibility of change for them – this is not a category they will necessarily live out forever. Secondly, referring to the situation rather than the person opens up the consideration of the structural reasons for particular issues rather than an individual blaming approach, such as the prevalence of gangs on a particular estate. Thirdly, referring neutrally to the situation, for example 'gang affected', allows for other aspects of that situation to be seen, such as the positive experiences of social connectedness to the gang. School teachers have a mantra that 'the child is not the behaviour' to help them remember that negative behaviour is a sign of something else and does not mean a 'bad child'. Our equivalent as participatory researchers is to remember that the issue is not the person and many factors lead to people experiencing certain situations; they are not 'bad people making bad choices'.

Further to this, many researchers, policymakers and practitioners refer to people as 'vulnerable' or 'at risk'. These labels are well intentioned but also problematic. The label of vulnerable itself, or of different types of vulnerability, has negative connotations which can reduce an individual's sense of empowerment and agency. A good test for language is whether you would use it directly with that person and how you would feel if someone referred to you in that way. We can't imagine ever calling someone 'vulnerable' – who are we to deem them so, and what impact will that labelling have on them? A second issue with the language of 'vulnerability' and 'at risk' is that the labels mask complex, interwoven issues that affect people's lives. Whilst someone might be 'at risk' of domestic abuse, they might also be a dedicated and effective parent. A single term rarely describes a person wholly. Thirdly, these labels lump everyone together under one stereotype which will hide a wide range of variety between people and their situations; it is therefore inaccurate. Further, the term encourages black-and-white thinking as 'vulnerable' or 'not vulnerable' and does not encourage an understanding of the dynamic and nuanced layers or levels of vulnerability. Finally, vulnerability is a cultural phenomenon. Sharing that you are part of the LGBTQIA+ community in one part of the world may not place anyone in any danger, but in others it could have life-threatening implications. The cultural context of any situation therefore needs to be taken into consideration, reinforcing our previous point that people are located in situations which define vulnerability rather than vulnerability being a 'thing' in its own right.

The takeaway message from this is that, as a participatory researcher recruiting co-researchers, or as a group of co-researchers recruiting participants, it is more inclusive to refer to people by the situations in which they find themselves in at any one point in time. Once they are engaged, they can determine how they wish to be referred to, removing the issue entirely as well as offering an opportunity for empowerment. Some examples of more (but not entirely) neutral references to groups of people as living in situations and having experiences are given in Table 6.1.

A final difficulty with terminology about participants is calling them 'hard to reach'. Of course, there are groups of people with whom we may not have regular contact, who we do not know very well and who may be reluctant to engage with research for a wide range of valid reasons. This does not make these people 'hard to reach'; we need to take the opposite view that the research is 'hard to engage with'. This fundamental restructuring of the sentence positions the responsibility and issue in the correct place. The issue is for the researchers and co-researchers to overcome,

Table 6.1: Finding situational labels rather than personal labels

Negative personal label	Situational or circumstantial label
Poor	Living in poverty
Drug user/alcoholic	Experiencing drug and/or alcohol issues
Excluded/isolated	Experiencing exclusion and/or isolation
Criminal	With experience of crime/incarceration
School failure	Experience of school failure
Ill	Living with an illness

not the potential participants. You may need to put previous conventions and norms to one side in order to enter the lifeworld of the co-researchers and participants; to connect with them in ways that are meaningful to them. We will say more about this in the recruitment section below.

Being attentive to language is a key skill for all researchers, and particularly participatory researchers. We need to use clean and neutral language that respects everyone maintaining an inclusive and engaging approach.

Sampling strategies

Many research books will talk about **sampling strategies,** so here we unpack what they mean and what your participatory sampling strategy might be as a group of co-researchers finding participants.

Sampling, in research terms, is identifying people who would be best suited to be involved in research. Most sampling strategies are focused on making sure the people involved are '**representative**' of the area of investigation. For example, sampling should not just include all the friends and colleagues we have ever had a cup of tea with, but also the people from different communities, organisations and social groups to ensure we have a conscious and inclusive mindset rather than exclusive and limited to only who/what we know.

A '**target population**' is the term used to describe all the people in the world who could be involved if you had limitless resources. This is where the use of situational or circumstantial labels is important. The '**sample**' is the group of people you will consciously and inclusively invite to take part. It's unlikely that you will be able to work with everyone in the world so you'll develop some rules of parameters to narrow it down. These could be by place, experience, demographic or some other factor. Having invited these people to take part, the ones who do say yes are then called '**participants**'.

The '**sampling strategy**' is the process of putting these rules or parameters in place in order to narrow down the sample. Let's imagine a scenario: you want to research how many people drink tea first thing in the morning. Your target group includes everyone who drinks tea in the world and you have narrowed this down further to everyone who drinks tea in the same town as you. Five sampling strategies are identified here as a starting point for your thinking.

Random sample: a random approach would pick people randomly from this group. You could choose every other household of tea drinkers for example. This would give you a random selection of people.

Stratified sample: this is where you want to ensure you reach certain groups of people, rather than leaving it to chance (as above), so you identify a range of groups. For example, a study may be keen to understand how age affects tea drinking, so you want people aged 20–40, 41–60, 61–80 and 81–100. This gives us four stratified groups. Whilst very strategic, it's a time-consuming approach to use.

Opportunity sampling: this does what it says, inviting anyone from the target population and accepting that those who say yes are the right people at that time and place. Whilst the most convenient of sampling strategies, it may mean only certain groups are included in the research and thus it may not be fully representative.

Purposive sampling: this means the researchers go out and purposefully find particular people who are available and who fit the target group. It means you select people you know of or who can identify as particularly valuable. This also relates to the power and interest matrix above.

Snowball sampling: this approach starts small and grows bigger like a rolling snowball. You initially recruit a small group of participants who then find another one or more participant each, and so on, so your sample gradually grows bigger and bigger. This might also be a good way to recruit co-researchers as word gets out that it's a great project to be involved in!

In our first case study example students snowballed as co-researchers coming together, and then their surveying of the whole school was opportunistic, with the risk that only certain age groups would be represented in the research and thus it may not be fully representative.

The parents' group and the practitioner group were both purposive in their targeting of their own established groups.

Chapter activity

Consider which other sampling strategies each of the three case studies could have adopted.

- Student-led research on mental health in school
- Community-led research on stop and search by police
- A multi-agency team researching how they work together

How many is 'enough'?

An age-old issue in research is working out how many people is 'enough' to be part of your project. A quantitative approach will seek large populations to create findings that can be generalised across society. A qualitative approach will be more content with small numbers of participants as long as there is more depth to the data gathered. A mixed-methods approach typically (but not always) looks to start more broadly with larger numbers or generalisable quantitative data and then narrow the sample size for deeper qualitative data.

As well as working out the number of participants you ideally want to meet your research aim, you may also need to consider practical issues. How many participants do you have access to? How many people in a particular group do you think will want to be involved? How much data does the team have time to analyse? These practicalities may override your ideal design – research is always a messy business! This is exemplified in different ways across all three of our case studies.

The group of students from group A wanted larger numbers, so they targeted the whole school. This brought up questions of how they were expecting to analyse large numbers of data, as well as whether they had large enough numbers to generalise from in relation to the broader national data they were interested in relating their study to?

The group of parents from group B wanted smaller numbers of more in-depth experiences. This brought up questions of whether only the vocal, confident participants would speak up – how would they also hear the unheard voices they valued so much?

The group of practitioners from group C wanted their individual teams to engage in multiple elements of the research. This brought up questions of complexity – what if some of the participants bought into some parts of the research and not others?

These examples highlight how very different sampling strategies might be and the complications that exist in all research projects.

Recruitment strategies

Working out how to approach everyone is vitally important and different approaches may be needed for different types of participants. Getting the 'offer right' is important, not so that you can coerce people into taking part but so that they can really judge whether they want to be a part of your project or not. The language you use is one key aspect of this – pitching the invitation in the right way takes careful consideration. The way in which people are invited is another concern. Some people may want an official letter of invitation, whereas others might respond better to an informal chat and every mode of communication in between.

How you reach people is also important. You might be able to approach some people because you know them, but others might need to be reached through other contacts or organisations. Typically, in participatory research the co-researchers are the gatekeepers to accessing people that you as the participatory researcher may have never had access to – this is one of the greatest gifts of participatory research, as is apparent across all three of our case studies. However, this is not always the case; sometimes you may be the gatekeeper to populations the co-researchers would not have been able to access, or indeed you may all be starting from scratch.

For some people, being reached via a trusted contact is important whereas others may be happy to receive a random letter, email, social media post or phone call out of the blue. Weighing up all the possibilities and making your best guess at how to approach people is an important part of the research process.

A further issue is that 'research' may not appeal to everyone. Previous experiences of research or researchers may have convinced people they won't participate. For example, we have negative experiences of market researchers cold calling and spam emailing or getting pop-ups on our web browsers to rate yet another product or company's service. Understanding different perceptions of research is therefore important. Research might remind people of schools and education which may not necessarily be a positive experience for them, and so making clear why their experiences are valued, what the research will involve and how you will make it accessible and meaningful is another important factor to communicate.

The key message from this is how, as a group of co-researchers, you consider every aspect of your target sample population and what that might mean for recruiting them into the research. As a participatory researcher, this section should help you to support the co-researchers to be able to vary the approach by group or even by person and be ready to be flexible and try a range of different approaches.

Dealing with drop out

Finally, let's be honest, life is complex and dynamic and, as such, co-researchers and participants may not all be able to participate throughout the research project. One of the guiding ethical principles of research (see Chapter 10) is that anyone is free to withdraw from the research at any time and this needs to be made clear to everyone and implemented in a non-judgmental way.

You might want to talk about this as a group of co-researchers at the start of the project so you know when, or which parts of the project, everyone is available. Life sometimes throws us unforeseen circumstances too and so co-researchers may have to leave the project for a wide range of reasons. It may also be that the reality of being involved does not match their expectations, or they are not enjoying working on the project. Having strong relationships with the co-researchers will mean you can have open conversations about participation and deal with issues that come up.

You might want to engage more people in the research than is really needed to allow for people leaving the project, but don't overstretch what is possible. And all of this applies to co-researchers considering their sample sizes and make-up.

Reflective task and tea break six

- How did you experience the tasks of creating a map of all your stakeholders and mapping them into the power and influence matrix?
- What did you learn about your project?
- What did you learn about potential participants?
- What did you learn about yourself?

Summary

This chapter has discussed who could be involved in participatory research, how and in what ways. We have discussed this in terms of recruiting co-researchers as well as how to support co-researchers to recruit participants. We discussed different people's interests and notions of power and provided a reminder of the importance of empowerment as a core process within participatory research. Issues of labelling have been highlighted as significant along with the efforts you can go to in order to give everyone the best chance to participate in the project. We ended with more practical information on a range of sampling strategies and recruitment ideas, as well as dealing with drop out.

Further reading

- This paper by Florencia Luna is a great insight into the issues of 'vulnerability' as a label: Luna, F. (2019) 'Identifying and evaluating layers of vulnerability – a way forward', *Developing World Bioeth*, 19: 86–95. https://doi.org/10.1111/dewb.12206
- The following texts focus specifically on working with young people in research contexts: Tisdall, E., Davis, J. and Gallagher, M. (2009) *Researching with Children and Young People*, London: Sage.
- Heath, S., Brooks, R., Cleaver, E. and Ireland, E. (2009) *Researching Young People's Lives*, London: Sage.
- And these focus on working with people with additional needs: Barton, J. and Hayhoe, S. (2021) *Emancipatory and Participatory Research for Emerging Educational Researchers. Theory and Case Studies of Research in Disabled Communities*, London: Routledge.
- Goodley, D. (2016) *Disability Studies: An Interdisciplinary Introduction* (2nd edn), London: Sage.
- This website provides an overview of the process of empowerment in our model of wellbeing development: https://aca-wellbeing.com/, or you can read more in our book.
- This paper by Powers and Tiffany discusses learning from four examples of participatory youth research and evaluation: https://www.health.ny.gov/community/youth/development/docs/jphmp_s079-s087.pdf

- This technical paper by Otado et al. highlights the importance of cultural competence when recruiting people to research projects: https://www.ncbi.nlm.nih.gov/pmc/articles/PMC4626379/

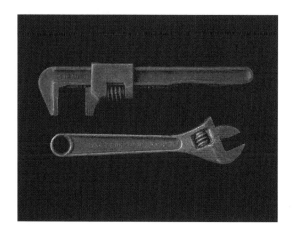

7

How shall we collect our data?

Chapter overview

This chapter provides an overview of common data collection tools and details the tools that are particularly good at promoting participation. We will discuss the tensions inherent in 'training' co-researchers in a range of data collection tools in order for them to best decide what to use and suggest a range of resources you might need to support their training.

What are data collection tools?

A toolbox usually has a range of different tools inside such as hammers, spanners, wrenches and pliers, all designed for a specific job. Sometimes you get different sized tools for different sized tasks, for example sledgehammers for heavy building work and small hammers for hanging pictures. Researchers also have a toolbox with a range of practical ways to collect data. Just like the physical tools, data collection tools are all designed for different types and sizes of job. The term data collection tool therefore just refers to a way of collecting data. Every physical tool and data collection tool will have a range of advantages and disadvantages which help you decide which job it is best suited to.

This chapter will look at some common data collection tools, discussing their uses, advantages and disadvantages and design considerations. Because each data collection tool has so many variations, the discussion will be very general, providing a simple overview. You may need to do some more reading, hence the more extensive list of further reading at the end of this chapter.

Common data collection tools

When we ask new groups of co-researchers 'what is research?' and 'what do researchers do?' we are usually told they do experiments and surveys. This gives us an insight into the most visible forms of research in Western society. It is highly unlikely you will be doing a scientific experiment with your co-researchers, so we will start with surveys as one of the most common forms of research we encounter in our daily lives.

Surveys

Surveys allow researchers to collect data from a large number of people in a controlled and practical manner. Surveys might be conducted on hard-copy printouts, online or verbally in person. Deciding what format is the most appropriate depends on who and where you will be doing the surveying. Literacy is a key factor in whether a hard copy or online survey will work, as is the ability to write or access the internet. Verbal surveys can overcome this issue to some extent and many online survey maker tools now have the option to read the questions aloud to participants.

There are a plethora of online survey maker tools, many of which have a free basic package. They often have suggestions for questions and types of responses as well as designs, themes, colours and fonts. They are also compatible with multiple devices (computer, tablet, phone). And one of the greatest advantages of online surveys is they often do some basic data analysis for you, turning this into infographics and/or collating data into a spreadsheet for you, saving your data input time (analysis is discussed further in Chapter 8).

Surveys can include a wide range of question types. As surveys are usually used to collect data from a lot of people the options for answers are often (but not always) quantitative. The following question types are examples of types of closed questions that are very common and all generate quantitative and numeric data:

- Single or multiple-choice questions allow a respondent to tick one or more options to show which are relevant or important to them.
- Scaling questions allow a respondent to show how significant or important something is to them.
- A rating scale allows respondents to show how large or small something is.
- A ranking question allows respondents to put items in order of preference.

What results from the analysis of these types of questions is a count of how many people indicated a particular type of answer. However, it is impossible to know why they provided that answer. Further, these types of questions rely on the researcher knowing what options are relevant to respondents. If someone finds none of the options are relevant it can prevent them from answering or even continuing the survey. Some of this can be overcome by adding some kind of 'not applicable' option. It is also possible to have an 'other' box with space to add new options not listed by the researcher. These are called **open-ended** questions and allow the respondent to write what they like – sometimes these responses have a word or space limit. These types of questions give people a chance to say what they want and how they want and are often used as a qualitative 'tell me why you provided that answer' in addition to the quantitative questions above. Whilst this provides rich qualitative data, it is not as straightforward to analyse as the quantitative data and will need **coding** (discussed in Chapter 8) before it can be reported.

In summary, surveys are best used with larger sample sizes and most commonly provide numerical data to quantitative questions.

Survey design tips:

- Limit the number of questions;
- Check the language is appropriate;
- Check the questions flow from one to another;
- Make sure there are options to capture other, not applicable and non-responses;
- Ask someone to pilot the survey so you can see how long it takes them and get feedback from them.

The students within group A from our case studies used the United Kingdom's Office for National Statistics' (ONS) three wellbeing questions because The Children's Society have said they are reliable and suitable for use with young people over the age of eight. The questions were:

- Overall, how satisfied are you with your life nowadays?
- Overall, to what extent do you feel that the things you do in your life are worthwhile?
- Overall, how happy did you feel yesterday? (ONS, 2021)

These three questions were rated on a scale of 0 (not at all) to 10 (completely). The students also added an open question at the end that asked: 'what has the biggest impact at school on your wellbeing?'.

The practitioners in group C approached this slightly differently to the students: they asked a set of survey questions before and after the focus groups as they wanted to see if there was any change. Their questions centred on the effectiveness of different elements of their multi-agency working such as collaboration, decision making, sharing information and resource management.

Interviews

Interviews sound very formal and may bring to mind someone being asked lots of questions by someone in power! However, interviews may often be an informal conversation with a research participant. Some participants like to be invited to an interview as it sounds important and others would be really deterred by the word. Interviews are well suited to exploring a topic in detail, one to one, with a smaller sample of people. It is a time-consuming process and that makes it unsuitable for mass research.

Interviews collect verbal data. This might be written down in note form or audio or video recorded. It is difficult to maintain eye contact with a participant, listen, think of the next suitable question and write notes – so recording an interview can help with this. However, the presence of a recording device might completely deter some participants. For example, we've been told by young people in the past that recording an interview reminded them of being taken to a police station – this was definitely not the environment we were trying to recreate!

We are all more and more used to conference and video calls – mainly catalysed through the COVID-19 pandemic. This has opened up the opportunity to interview people across the globe. People can have cameras on or off and they can be easily recorded (with permission).

There are three broad approaches to interviewing or having conversations – structured, semi-structured and unstructured.

In a **structured** interview, a range of questions are pre-determined by the researcher and these are adhered to without any deviation. Whilst this ensures the process is identical for all participants, it can make the interview feel very formal and at times jarring as you ask the next question no matter what the participant said last.

A **semi-structured** approach can help with this, as a set of key questions are identified beforehand but they can be asked in any order, additional questions can be added and the researcher can have a more natural, flowing discussion with the participant.

Finally, there is the **unstructured** approach where an interviewer might introduce a broad topic and then ask the participant what they think about it, leaving them to decide what to include and what to leave out. This approach might be useful for sensitive topics as the researcher does not pry into anything more than is welcomed. However, some participants might find it too vague and it might not provide the researchers with the data they were looking for.

Interview design tips:

- Test out your questions on a few different people to see how easily understood they are.
- Check out whether participants are comfortable with recording the interview before you meet them.
- Be relaxed and natural; try to build a rapport with the participant before you dive into the questions.
- Find somewhere quiet and undisturbed to undertake the interviews (whether face to face or virtual with voice or video call).

The parents in group B from our case studies used semi-structured interviews with each other. They wanted some structure to follow as there would be multiple researchers conducting interviews, but also wanted to allow for the interview to flow in a natural direction where possible.

Focus groups

Focus group is a term that has emerged from market research where groups of people are asked to come together to focus on a product, providing feedback to the marketers. In effect a focus group is a group interview or group conversation. The advantage of a group interview is that you can get more people's views at the same time so it can be more time efficient than interviewing. Another strength of the focus group is that group members can bounce ideas off one another, promoting wider and deeper data for the researcher and perhaps some learning for the group. A disadvantage is that it can be difficult to know how many people agree with any one statement, and powerful people may dominate the conversation. Some participants may feel safer speaking in a group setting than individually; for others the reverse will be true. 'Group think', or everyone saying the same thing when they would not individually, can also occur. These factors mean that knowing the focus group participants and how they are likely to interact may be important. Another consideration is how your participants would like to work. You may be able to offer the choice of an individual interview or a focus group.

As with the interviews, the researcher could take a structured, semi-structured or unstructured approach to a focus group. However, an unstructured focus group obviously has the risk of going off topic. And as with interviews, there is the choice of whether to take notes and audio or video record the session. You can also do focus groups virtually using a conference/video call that can again be recorded easily, with permission.

Focus group design tips:

- limit numbers so everyone has a chance to speak;
- do some icebreakers so people get used to talking before the data collection begins;
- identify some strategies to manage particularly talkative and quiet people;
- decide how you will deal with any heated disagreement in a session.

The practitioners in group C from our case studies carried out focus groups to explore perceptions of multi-agency working within their individual teams, as this fitted well with their desire for team development.

Observations

Observations are useful when there is a particular behaviour that is the focus of research. For example, if people choose a cup or mug to drink their tea out of at a tea shop. In general, an observation involves a researcher watching how people behave (what they say and do). In small settings you would need consent from everyone to be observed – a common critique of observation is that people change their behaviour when they know they are being watched. Observations at a population level (for example, in the high street) cannot gain the consent of everyone there, but must instead be conducted in plain view rather than hidden or by stealth. Observations are most used in anthropological and ethnographic research where the researchers are trying to identify key features of a particular culture or phenomenon.

A second limitation of observations is that they only provide data on what people do or say; they do not provide any insight into what people are thinking or what they believe – the motivations for what they say and do are therefore unknown. Observations can be highly structured with record sheets and frequency counts, semi-structured with particular behaviour to notice (as present or absent) or unstructured. Observations are recorded by the researcher using digital or physical means. They are usually sat somewhere they can see what is happening, in sight of the participants, but as unobtrusively as possible.

Observational design tips:

- Work out how to introduce the research, and your presence, to the participants.
- Decide what you are observing and how you can capture that most easily.
- Work out where to position yourself so you can see, but you are not in the way.
- Capture the context or setting where the behaviours are taking place – this is often significant.
- Remember to look up and observe what is happening as well as look down to take notes.

Secondary data

Data you collect yourself, such as what we have described so far, is called **primary data**. **Secondary data**, however, is data that already exists in the world that has been collected by someone else. For example, many countries have a national office that collects population-wide statistics. This can be a useful source of data to explore questions. The benefit of using secondary data is that it saves a lot of researcher time. Secondary data might also include other reports and research studies conducted on the same topic. The findings from these can be used as a type of data themselves. This links back to the section in Chapter 3 about locating your study in the wider literature and might be worth rereading to refresh your thinking.

The students in group A did a great deal of secondary data analysis, looking into the ONS wellbeing questions and the wider statistics on young people's mental health internationally.

The major limitation of secondary data is that it was not collected with your question in mind and so may not be a perfect fit. Several sources of data might conflict with one another which can also be problematic. Access can also be an issue – sometimes you can access summary statistics (for example, 80 per cent of young people are happy) but you cannot access the raw data that led to the summary statement. That may or may not be an issue for you depending on your question.

Tips for using secondary data:

- Work out why the data was first collected and how close that purpose is to your research.
- Check whether you can access all the raw data or just the analysis of summary statistics.
- Evaluate the quality and reliability of the data.
- Check when the data was collected and whether it is recent enough for your purpose.
- When you have decided what you will use, take one piece of data at a time and work out what it is telling you rather than tackling it all at once.

Creative data collection tools

All researchers hope that people will participate in their research but, from the limitations discussed above, you will note that some people might not want to write, talk or be watched. So, what more engaging and creative tools are there to support people to participate in research?

Storytelling

Telling your personal story can be a very different experience to answering questions. Some people call this narrative research. Many research participants report that it is a validating experience to be listened to when telling a life story. However, for other people it may be too personal or painful to recount. Storytelling can be a written or verbal process or could be aided by drawing pictures or selecting images from a bank. These can be arranged in a timeline or in significance, or however suits the participant.

Again, recording the story – in photos, notes, audio or video – is a key consideration.

Because stories tend to be long and detailed they can create a high workload for the researchers analysing them. This needs to be considered. One of their prime strengths is that the participant has much more control of the situation, what they say and how they choose to present it. Some researchers critique storytelling as too subjective – however, participatory researchers are searching for those subjective accounts of the world and so this is not problematic.

Storytelling might be particularly relevant to certain age groups – younger and older adults for example, or particular cultures. Aboriginal and Torres Strait Islander peoples, for example, regularly 'yarn' stories, and so yarning is a culturally appropriate way to generate knowledge. Stories, poems and raps may all be useful ways for people to express themselves.

Design tips for storytelling sessions:

- How can you get people started – where will they be comfortable telling their story? What prompts might they need?
- When and how would you encourage someone to say more? When and how would you interrupt someone?
- How will you capture the story?

The parents in group B from our case studies found that some of their interviews turned into storytelling, either during the interview or at a later date when participants shared more detail via a second interview or by writing their story down.

Photo or object elicitation

Sometimes images and objects are more powerful than a memory. Photovoice supports research participants to have more control over their data and to have increased voice. The process involves the participants taking photographs of things that are important to them and related to the research topic. It might be 'where I make tea'. The participants could take photos of their kitchen and all the equipment they use to make tea. These photos would then be viewed by the co-researcher and participant together, providing them with a shared image to discuss. This can sometimes promote more dialogue, and therefore data, than a set of questions alone might have generated, and is often called 'photo elicitation'. Consideration needs to be given to how the participants will take pictures – will they use a disposable camera, a digital camera or their phone? These are all practical matters to think through and are perhaps the biggest drawback of the tool – its obvious dependence on equipment.

Objects can be used to a similar effect. A participant could be asked to show their favourite cup or mug – and that item would then be a prompt for a discussion about tea. Any object would work and might be more accessible than a photograph depending on its size and value! Sometimes this tool is called 'object elicitation' as the use of an object elicits more dialogue.

Photo and object elicitation design tips:

- What equipment will you need to capture and share the photographs?
- Will the participants need photography skills?
- Will a photograph or object capture something of relevance to the research question?

Walking research

Taking this approach one step further, some researchers will literally go for a walk with a participant who can show them all the things that are important or relevant to them in their community. This could be recorded on a video camera, the conversation could be recorded on an audio device or notes could be made by the researcher at a later date. Even if the research question is not exploring a place, it might be that the process of walking side by side enables a conversation to develop and flow more naturally than sitting next to each other. Its process can therefore be powerful in aiding participation, particularly for people who may struggle to sit still for a length of time.

This could have been a very powerful tool with the parents' group case study.

Walking research design tips:

- Where will you go – anywhere, or a set route?
- How long will you be out for?
- Do you have the right gear for bad weather?
- How will you record the walking research?

Mapping tools

Diagrams might be a more appropriate way for participants to convey what they have to say to a researcher. A wide range of visual mapping tools exist that can help. This could literally be a map – of an area or community, hand drawn or a purchased map that is annotated. Similarly, participants might want to draw network maps showing who knows who or how ideas connect (a mind map). Diagrams might be helpful in portraying information – route maps, flow diagrams, pro and con diagrams – and might unlock additional meaning for participants and can be done individually or in a group. In addition, you will have an artefact – a diagram. You will need to consider whether the diagram alone is a good enough piece of data, or whether you need to capture some conversation about it too, in a similar way to photo or object elicitation.

Mapping tool design tips:

- What resources will you need?
- Will you need any prompts or examples?
- Can everyone involved see the diagram?
- Who gets to hold the pen/s?
- What do you do if they make a mistake and want to start again?

The practitioners in group C from our case studies did individual value maps, which participants then shared within the focus groups and merged to come up with a team value map.

Arts-based tools

A wide range of arts tools exist which can be used for data collection. These include drawing, collage, painting, drama, dance, singing/songwriting, poetry/rap, puppetry, sculpture, modelling and so on. Participants do not need to be skilled in any of these creative arts but rather just enjoy engaging in them. Working creatively can promote a deeper level of reflection about the research topic and can produce richer data. Many of these techniques could be used by most people as we have been familiar with them as children, for example drawing stick figures, playing with plasticine or construction blocks. Whilst our familiarity with them might make many of them accessible, they may also be deemed too 'childish' by some participants. Some arts-based tools may operate at a more professional level and involve facilitation from an expert, for example in recording a rap or creating a drama production. The time and resources available may be a limiting factor in using arts-based creative data collection tools.

As with other participatory methods, you will need to consider whether the artefact itself (the poem, artwork, dance) is enough, or whether it needs a commentary or explanation alongside it. Another issue is artistic block. Some people do not want to engage in arts-based methods as they believe they are no good at them and may be laughed at for trying, or they may think they are not serious enough to be 'proper' research. Yet again, understanding the participants and knowing what will work for them is of vital importance.

Arts-based tool design tips:

- What will participants feel comfortable doing?
- Can they all participate?
- What equipment and space do you need?
- Do you need any expert input/facilitation?
- Will the artefact stand on its own or do you need a dialogue about it?
- Who gets to keep the artefact, them or you?

Whilst we have positioned creative and arts methods as 'tools' within participatory research, it is also important to note that arts-based research is a distinct strand of research in and of itself, but this is beyond the scope of this book to explore – there are further signposts in the further reading below if you want to know more.

Digital tools

Many online tools now exist to enable people to work together even if they are not in the same space, and these can be useful for researchers too. Some participants might be willing to take part in research as long as they don't have to meet anyone. Some may be unable to join a research project physically due to where they live or their situation (for example, prison facilities) or due to health issues or the expense of travel.

The simplest digital tools include email, video calls/online meetings and numerous digital survey generators. Social media also provides us with an array of ways to reach and engage with people. Aside from these, there is a wide range of online workspaces, project boards and whiteboards that people can add to, both individually or collaboratively with multiple users, and in live sessions or in their own time. Participants can type or draw or upload items (examples include Miro, Mural, jamboards and Padlet, to name but a few). Many of these have no cost or low-cost versions and can all be accessed via numerous devices (laptop, tablet or phone). The key consideration in working digitally are issues with people's connectivity and data allowances. The skills to be able to navigate a digital project might also be a deterrent. And, for some people, working online itself may put them off participating.

Digital tool design tips:

- Can everyone access the tool?
- Can everyone use the tool?
- How intuitive is the tool?
- How secure is the tool?
- How can you extract data from the tool?

There was mixed use of digital tools within our case studies.

The students in group A used a mix of hard-copy surveys and online surveys in order to make them as accessible as possible to participants. They gained permission for the digital surveys to be completed on school computers during breaktimes, registration and IT classes, as well as in their own time on their own devices.

The parents in group B used video calls as well as in-person interviews.

The practitioners in group C used online surveys (because of their team's daily use of digital tools) as well as video conference calls and an online project board to keep in touch with each other throughout the duration of the project and because of their geographical spread and worry about keeping motivation and momentum.

Supporting participants to choose data collection tools

Ideally the co-researchers will decide how to conduct the research. In order to decide which data collection tool to use, they will need to know a little bit about each one. Your role might be to provide them with access to that information. It may be difficult to know how many to introduce them to and how much to tell them about each one. On one hand, with minimal understanding and knowledge they may choose data collection tools they are most familiar with but which are perhaps not most suited to the project. On the other hand, knowing everything about every tool might be onerous and overwhelming. Additionally, they may introduce a tool you have never heard of – this might be particularly the case with digital tools that are developing all the time. In which case you can explore its suitability together.

You will need to decide how to navigate these tensions with the group and that is the reflective task at the end of this chapter.

The second decision co-researchers have to make is which tools to use. This will be a group decision and everyone might have a different view or preference. The guiding principle for the decision is what will be the best experience for the participants *and* generate the data we need. By 'best experience' we mean the most fun, engaging, meaningful, safest and appropriate tool. If you are researching across a diverse group, this might even mean using different tools with different groups.

Reflective task and tea break seven

Consider how much about data collection tools the co-researchers will need to know.

- How many tools do you think they need to know about?
- How much detail will they need to know about each?
- What is the best way for them to learn about them?
- How will you all know when you know enough?

Summary

This chapter has given an overview of different data collection tools. We've reviewed a range of common data collection tools, as well as a range of creative tools that can be particularly engaging in participatory research. A key challenge in participatory research is how much time to dedicate to training co-researchers, and how much time they have to learn about tools in order to make a decision on what to use, as well as how to use it.

Further reading

- Whilst a generic rather than participatory research book, David Gray's text gives a good overview of each of the main tools in research: Gray, D. (2009) *Doing Research in the Real World*, London: Sage.

- Practical guide to surveys: https://www.mitre.org/sites/defa ult/files/pdf/05_0638.pdf
- A thorough text on interviews can be found here: Kvale, S. and Brinkmann, S. (2009) *Interviews. Learning the Craft of Qualitative Research Interviewing*, London: Sage.
- Or this is a good practical online guide to interviews: https://www. tandfonline.com/doi/full/10.1080/0142159X.2018.1497149
- Here is a practical guide to focus groups: https://www.ngo connect.net/sites/default/files/resources/A%20Step-by-Step%20Guide%20to%20Focus%20Group%20Research.pdf
- This is an online practical guide to secondary data: http://r2ed. unl.edu/presentations/2011/RMS/120911_Koziol/120911_Koziol.pdf
- Clandinin and Connelly offer the definitive guide to narrative research: Clandinin, D. and Connelly, F. (2000) *Narrative Inquiry*, San Francisco, CA: Jossey Bass.
- And here is an in-depth online guide to narratives: https:// www.keele.ac.uk/media/keeleuniversity/facnatsci/schpsych/ documents/counselling/conference/5thannual/NarrativeAppr oachestoCaseStudies.pdf
- Practical guide to photovoice: https://rpay.link/guide/ pdf20.pdf
- Practical guide to mapping tools: http://hummedia.manches ter.ac.uk/schools/soss/morgancentre/toolkits/2008-07-tool kit-participatory-map.pdf
- Practical guide to walking methods: https://www.bera. ac.uk/blog/walking-interviews-a-participatory-resea rch-tool-with-legs
- Practical guide to digital tools: https://www.researchgate.net/ publication/333641756_Doing_Digital_Methods
- If you are interested in knowing more about the arts-based approach to research, this is an essential text: Barone, T. and Eisner, E. (2011) *Arts Based Research*, London: Sage.
- This is a very practical guide to creative methods: Mannay, D. (2016) *Visual, Narrative and Creative Research Methods. Application, reflection and ethics*, London: Routledge.
- And here is a practical online guide to arts-based methods: https:// social-change.co.uk/files/Knowledge_Hub_-_Creative_Resea rch_Methods.pdf

8

What do we do with our data?

Chapter overview

This chapter introduces data analysis. This can seem the most daunting part of research for some people but it doesn't have to be. For this reason, this chapter will give a very straightforward overview of analysis to get you started on how to analyse the main types of data you are likely to have, namely numbers, words and images. We will also remind you of the socially just principles of participatory research, and thus participatory analysis, to keep our feet on the ground!

What is data analysis?

Data analysis simply means how you make sense of the data you have collected. This involves looking for patterns and trends in the information you have collected so that you can best summarise what it has to tell you – its story.

As human beings we are generally skilled at looking for patterns. As young children we used to collect and sort objects into groups of different sizes, shapes and colours. Looking at data uses just the same skills – finding commonality and difference in the data you have collected and sorting it into different groups.

Sorting through information and deciding whether things are the same or different might differ from person to person and study to study. Imagine you are sorting tea into different categories. One person might put all black teas into one group, all fruit teas into another and herbals into a third. Someone else might sort them by country of origin, or by soaking time. The way we approach analysis can therefore differ. We could have many different sets of analysis and findings from one set of data. It is therefore important to discuss different ideas for how to do the analysis and different views of what that analysis shows within the group of co-researchers.

It is best to approach analysis with curiosity and an open mind, to discuss differences and to be aware that you could tell many different 'stories' from the data. Working out which is the most important or most appropriate story to tell will be a key discussion.

Qualitative and quantitative data

To start with, let's remember that we're already familiar with the two broad types of data: quantitative, number-based data and qualitative, language-based or image-based data. Whilst quantitative data refers to anything that is a pure number, qualitative data is more diverse and can include any word-based data (verbal or written) as well as images and pictures.

Approaching the data

There are three ways you can approach looking at (sorting through) the data. These are detailed in the table below (Table 8.1).

Yet again, it is important to point out that none of the three approaches to data analysis are better or worse than the other; each is tailored differently to suit different data so finding alignment between the research question, data collected and analytical approach is important.

Let's apply this broadly to our case studies:

Group A could analyse their data through the first approach: wider data says there is a drop in mental health gradually throughout school ages, particularly at age 14, and by 2 points in a 10-point scale. Can we see this trend in our data (approach one)?

Group B could analyse their data through the second approach: keeping an open mind and wondering what our data tells us about parents' experiences of their children being stopped and searched (approach two).

Group C could analyse their data through the third approach: first they searched for improvements in the before and after survey data and secondly they read through the focus group data searching for the barriers and enablers of multi-agency working (approach three).

Table 8.1: Approaches to data analysis

	Approach one	Approach two	Approach three
Description	This is used when you know what you are looking for and you go and look for it within the data	This is when you let the data speak for itself	In simple terms, this is a combination of approach one and two (in reality, it's more complicated!)
Research term	Deductive analysis	Inductive analysis	Abductive analysis

Quantitative analysis

So, let's get into the details. **Quantitative analysis** is about quantifying something. Examples of this include defining how much, how many, how often, how big and so on. Central to this approach, therefore, is counting and measuring. The quantitative approach is more commonly referred to as statistical analysis that produces (you've guessed it!) statistics.

There are different types of statistics and therefore different types of statistical analysis. We are going to keep things very straightforward here and talk about **descriptive statistics**. These describe, or summarise, the numerical data. If you like what you read, and want to know more, then we've written in more detail in our other book (Stuart, Maynard and Rouncefield, 2015).

To start, and most commonly, we will work out the '**average**' of a set of numbers. For example, what the average age of a tea drinker is. There are three different types of average. In this example, we could add up all the ages of tea drinkers and divide them by the total number of people in the group to find the '**mean**' age. This is most commonly what is meant by an 'average' age. However, we could also refer to the most common age of tea drinker by doing a tally of all the ages and seeing which is the most frequent. This is called the '**mode**' or most popular. The third way of working out the average would be to put all the ages in order and to look at the age that falls exactly halfway through the data set – that would be called the '**median**'. The median is not used very often in participatory research, so the mean and mode will be the best tools in your analytical toolbox.

Sometimes the **relative** quantity is important. For example, how many people drink decaffeinated tea compared to (or relative to) caffeinated tea. Other quantitative tools are useful here such as percentages, fractions and ratios. For example, 20 per cent of people drink decaffeinated tea, or a 5th, or 1 in 5 people.

Sometimes the **range** of answers in a data set is important. For example, if we were exploring how old tea drinkers were, it would be useful to indicate the youngest through to the oldest person; the age of tea drinkers ranged between 8 and 102 years of age.

We can explore each of these through groups A and C in our case studies, as they both used quantitative analysis.

Group A could look for the range of student ages who responded (for example, the range of ages of student responses was 11–18 years); the average (mean) wellbeing score (for example, the average, or mean, wellbeing score was 6 on a 10-point scale); the lowest-scoring age group relative to the other ages (for example, the lowest scoring age group was 15-year-olds); and then look at the scores relative to ONS data (for example, the average wellbeing score for this group was lower than the national average in the ONS data).

Group C could look for a change in the 'after' score relative to the 'before' score (for example, 80 per cent of the teams showed an improved score); the range of changes on the 10-point scale (for example, between 4 and 8 points of improvement); and the average (mode) change score (for example, +5 points of improvement).

Quantitative data analysis software packages and spreadsheets

There are lots of other types of statistical analysis, as well as the basic descriptive analysis that we have outlined here. Remember, if you want to know more, you can follow up with some of the further reading suggestions below.

Most descriptive statistics can be analysed through a spreadsheet (the most common being Excel). In fact, most online survey generators transfer responses straight into a spreadsheet for you to download and carry out analysis. Whilst this really cuts down manually entering data into the spreadsheet, you still have to analyse it. We don't want to state the obvious here (but we're going to anyway!) but, once your data is in a spreadsheet, you need to highlight the relevant data and click on 'insert formula' and the programme will do most of the basics we've described here. You can find out more about basic descriptive analysis on a spreadsheet. There are lots of quantitative data analysis software packages, such as SPSS Statistics, which could help you with more complicated analysis but these need more specialist skills and would need to be purchased.

We will return to tea to explore the use of descriptive statistics more fully. Table 8.2 is a data set about global tea consumption (Statista, 2020).

Table 8.2: Annual global tea consumption per capita

Ranking	Country	Annual tea consumption per capita in kgs
1	Turkey	3.16
2	Ireland	2.19
3	United Kingdom	1.94
4	Iran	1.50
5	Russia	1.38
6	Morocco	1.22
7	New Zealand	1.19
8	Chile	1.19
9	Egypt	1.01
10	Poland	1.00
11	Japan	0.97
12	Saudi Arabia	0.90
13	South Africa	0.81
14	Netherlands	0.78
15	Australia	0.75
16	Romania	0.73
17	United Arab Emirates	0.72
18	Germany	0.69
19	Hong Kong	0.65
20	Ukraine	0.58
21	China	0.57
22	Canada	0.51
23	Thailand	0.50
24	Malaysia	0.48
25	Indonesia	0.46
26	Switzerland	0.44
27	Czech Republic	0.42
28	Singapore	0.37
29	Slovakia	0.36
30	India	0.33

Source: Statista (2020)

Figure 8.1: Chart showing annual global tea consumption per capita

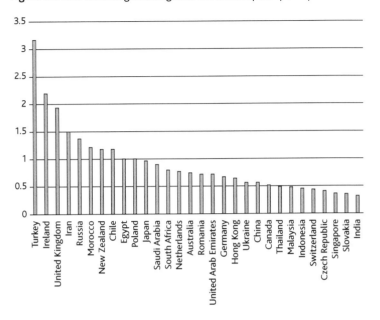

We can look at the highest and lowest amounts of tea consumption and state that: 'tea consumption is in the range of 0.33 to 3.16 kgs per capita per annum'.

We can add all the values up and divide them by the 30 countries to find the average (mean) amount of tea consumption. If you put the numbers in Excel and highlight them, the mean is automatically shown in the bottom bar. This will enable us to state: 'the mean tea consumption globally is 0.963 kg per capita per annum'.

We can also divide the top consumption (3.16 kgs for Turkey) by the lowest consumption (0.33 kg for India) to create a relative statement: 'Tea consumption is 9.5 times higher in Turkey than in India'.

We could also use an Excel spreadsheet to help us visualise the data in a chart. A simple bar chart is shown in Figure 8.1 as an example of this.

Qualitative analysis

How much tea is drunk in the world is a quantitative question, using quantitative data and a quantitative analytical approach.

Why tea is drunk in the world is a qualitative question, needing qualitative data and a qualitative approach. Qualitative analysis is about identifying different patterns in data. Rather than identifying how much or how big something is (quantifying it), it is interested in exploring what something is like – in myriad of different ways.

First thing's first you will want to have your data in front of you. This could be handwritten interview notes, observational notes, an audio or video recording or the transcript of a recording (we'll deal with visual data separately later in this chapter). Most researchers turn all audio recordings and the audio part of video recordings into written text in a process called '**transcription**' in order to make it visible for analysis. This is not compulsory; if the co-researchers were visually impaired, for example, there would be little point in transcription. Some co-researchers might prefer to listen to data and note down patterns rather than reading text, and so whether to transcribe or not is an important choice.

If you do decide to transcribe the data, there are multiple ways of going about it. You could complete a full or '**verbatim**' transcription of everything said, including pauses and 'erm's, or you could choose to do a partial transcription only typing up the sections that seem important. You can pay a professional to do this or use digital transcription software. Or you can do this yourself – whilst very time consuming, you will have a richer sense of the data than someone who did not collect it. Transcription is also essential with qualitative analysis software packages – detailed further below.

Different researchers talk about qualitative analysis in different ways. We are going to talk about it in terms of **coding** and **theming** the patterns you see in the data. This is the process of noticing different information and messages that stand out from the data. We then code these (think of this as giving them a code name or colour code) and then group them into themes.

Remember you can approach this in different ways: the message could emerge out of the data, you could go into the data looking for something specific or you could use a blend of both (inductive, deductive, abductive).

Let's look at some data from a blog about tea to see how this works. We read through the blog and then extracted the text below and highlighted (coded) words and sentences that had particular significance. We then re-read those bits and similar words and sentences were highlighted in bold and collated under the same code name within the table below. The headings in the table became our themes.

Of course, what I fell in love with initially was the **taste of the tea itself.** Despite the fact that it was essentially liquid sugar at the time, **I told myself this was my drink. Growing up in primarily a coffee-drinking household**, I stayed away from the bean and tea was something I would drink regularly and enjoy.

But going back to my first sip of tea – **a milky and sweet steep** from a strawberry flavoured black tea bag – I always knew it was **about so much more than the taste**. After all, I didn't have my very first cup of tea because I constantly heard people rave about how delicious it was.

No. **I actually had no idea if tea tasted good**.

I just knew it was something **grown ups always served when they got together**.

Instead, I had my very first cup just because I was finally at that age where **my parents let me have a little caffeine**. Remember the feeling when you finally get upgraded from the kids table to the adults table at family functions? That's exactly how I felt the day I was invited to join my mother and older sister's tea time. **For a seven-year-old, this felt like a rite of passage for me**.

So, you see, at seven years old **I didn't have people telling me 'tea is so delicious, just wait until you can try it!'** or 'there is nothing better than the taste of tea.' I had nothing to go off of and, looking back now, I was never fixated on how tea was going to taste, **I just wanted to join tea time!**

The tea's taste was just a vehicle from what I really experienced deep down … **a powerful connection with my mother and sister that was simply indescribable**. Tea makes me feel connected.

Watching my mom and sister having tea with one another I always knew there was a special bond that happened over their cups and I couldn't wait to experience that with them. **One of the greatest things about tea is how it brings people together**.

We could summarise from this thematic data analysis that there were four key themes that emerged from the data: sensory pleasure, wanting to be different, wanting to connect and tea as a rite of passage (Table 8.3). We would then have a heading for each one

Table 8.3: Example codes and themes

Sensory pleasure	Wanting to be different	Cultural significance: wanting to connect	Rite of passage
Taste of the tea itself	I told myself this was my drink. Growing up in primarily a coffee drinking household	About so much more than the taste	My parents let me have a little caffeine
A milky and sweet steep		Grown-ups always served when they got together	For a seven-year-old, this felt like a rite of passage for me
I actually had no idea if tea tasted good		I didn't have people telling me 'tea is so delicious, just wait until you can try it!'	
		I just wanted to join tea time!	
		A powerful connection with my mother and sister that was simply indescribable	
		One of the greatest things about tea is how it brings people together	

and describe the meaning that came out of the data with a quote, or quotes, provided as an example under each one.

Equally, we could have already had these themes and codes, perhaps from another study, and we could have looked at the data in search of them.

Either approach is qualitative in that it is describing why tea is significant to people. But here's where things get interesting; you can also quantify qualitative data by counting the number of examples within each theme/code. You need a larger sample size to be able to numerically generalise in this way though. If we had multiple blogs to analyse we might then be able to also count the number of times a particular code was mentioned, or refer to the percentage occurrence of each code, or even the most popular (mode) code. This is by no means necessary and it is often best to keep things simple. So, if the quantification does not add anything, don't do it.

Qualitative data analysis software packages and highlighter pens

Just as with quantitative data analysis, there are software packages (such as Quirkos, NVIVO and Atlas.ti) to help with analysing qualitative data. And just as with quantitative data there are more basic approaches – the highlighter pen or highlighter function in a Word document is the qualitative equivalent to the quantitative Excel spreadsheet.

The parents in group B from our case studies took the highlighter pen approach. They printed out interview transcripts and divided them up between them. As important messages started to emerge, they collectively allocated a colour code. As they started to collectively group these into themes, they cut out the text and stuck it on a large wall under the code name of the theme. This way they could all see it and the themes started to emerge.

Using software packages is quite straightforward and can save a lot of time. In very simple terms, you enter your data (usually a transcript) and ask the software to either find predefined codes or highlight common words and phrases for you. The practitioners in group C used a software package called Quirkos. They entered transcripts from their focus groups and searched for predefined codes that they had found from their reflections and created clusters of themes with them. They also searched for other common words and phrases that they may not have considered.

Visual data

Working with images and pictures uses a similar process in that the things depicted in an image can be coded. If we had asked people to photograph or draw the place where they make tea, I might note different things, for example the cup, saucer, kettle, spoon, tea bag, stove, mug, flask, loose tea and so on. This process is often described as '**visual analysis**'.

We asked Kaz to draw her thoughts about tea (yes, we actually did this!). Figure 8.2 below shows a number of icons which represent Kaz's thoughts about tea. Lucy then analysed this and gave them names such as 'warmth', 'comfort', 'friendship', 'rest'; alternatively they could be grouped together into themes such as 'emotional purpose' and 'varieties'. We could also ask Kaz about what she's drawn and she might tell us something we couldn't see, such as how she has linked each idea to the theme of tea with branches from a tea bush, showing that she considers tea to be an organic and growing plant. The images all show the ways tea nourishes her life; not only does it grow as a plant itself, it also supports Kaz's growth. Many other interpretations are also, of course, possible. You might like to consider what meaning you would draw from Figure 8.2.

The analysis of visual data does seem to be more contentious than any other forms of data. On one hand, some researchers argue it is unproblematic with a '**content analysis**' approach (Bell, 2000). On the other hand, some state that visual data cannot be analysed without an accompanying explanation of what the image-maker intended to show (Mannay, 2016). You will have to decide for yourself how to approach the analysis of visual images.

A summary of the different analytical approaches is provided in Table 8.4 below.

Developing a data analysis plan

Like many other aspects of research, the area of analysis is also full of choices. You will need to think about what data you have,

Figure 8.2: 'What tea means to me': example of visual data

Table 8.4: Types of qualitative and quantitative data analysis

Quantitative analysis	Qualitative analysis
Counting, tallying, frequency Percentages, fractions, ratios Range Average: mean, mode, median	Coding or thematic analysis Visual analysis Content analysis

what the best way to analyse it will be and how you will present that analysis. Woven throughout those choices is the question – what story do we want to tell?

We recommend looking at each of the pieces of data you have collected and coming up with a plan as to how you will analyse it. The questions in the headings of Table 8.5 might help guide this, enabling you to come up with your research storyline – you could turn this into a table or draw a mind map of your responses. Table 8.5 gives an example of the research plan for 'how tea creates unity in global communities'.

Table 8.5: Example of a data analysis plan

What have we got?	What type of data is it?	How will we analyse it?	How will that help us to build our story?
Survey of tea drinking	Age of participant	Count, range and mean	Helps to say who took part and how similar/diverse they are
	Country of origin	Count, range and mode	Helps to say which countries are represented and therefore how representative the results are
	Reason for drinking tea	Coding and themes Count, range and mode	Range of reasons for drinking tea and the most popular one
Interviews	How people prepare tea	Coding and themes	Range of ways tea is made
	Reason for drinking tea	Coding and themes	Rich range of reasons people drink tea
	Who people drink tea with	Range and mode	Range of people drink tea with

Participatory analysis

Traditionally analysis has always been the task of the skilled researcher. Even in research projects that claim to be co-produced or participatory, it is surprising to see how many researchers reclaim the analytical process. There may be a range of reasons for this. Perhaps the researcher does not want to make too many demands on the co-researchers by asking them to read, code and analyse the data. Perhaps the group has said they are not interested in analysis and would prefer the researcher to do it. A less positive motivation might be that the researcher does not think it is the co-researchers' job, or that they are not able to do it.

We firmly believe that co-researchers can be supported to do analysis. This is about remembering the central purpose of participatory research (inclusion, engagement, empowerment) and finding out what they are interested in saying. There are ways to make the process accessible and tools to facilitate collaborative analysis. Indeed, positivist researchers would concur that having multiple people doing the analysis adds quality to the process (although they may not value co-researchers as much as we do!).

Our task then, as participatory researchers, is to find ways to make analysis accessible, engaging, meaningful and rewarding.

We have introduced the concept of coding to co-researchers through sorting activities – literally playing with beans and buttons, then photos of objects and then text – building the complexity of the sorting task step by step. We also find making jigsaws is a fantastic metaphor for analysis. Everyone has a strategy for doing jigsaws (find the edges first) and a part they avoid (don't do the sky!). These translate well into analysis. How will we go about sorting the data (how do we find the edges)? How will we sort it (colour, shape, meaning)? Who will do which data set (sky, sea, trees)? What will we do with pieces that are missing – how much of the picture could be missing? What will we do if some pieces don't fit – how many of those would we ignore or include?

These creative and playful techniques can allow people to understand the process of analysis. Collaborative analysis in practice can be very different. Individuals could code the same thing and then compare results or groups could do the analysis jointly. Different people or groups could tackle different sections and then bring them together, or everyone could look at every piece of data. You could work together in a room with large pieces of paper or online using collaborative project boards. There are multiple choices in how your co-researchers decide to tackle the task.

Whilst we accept that not every participant will want to get involved in data analysis, we would like to stress the significance of them doing so. As data analysis is such an individual and subjective process, it is where a great deal of power resides. Whoever analyses the data will unconsciously superimpose their views of the world onto it. The analytical process is therefore prone to the reproduction of the views of the powerful in the world. For this reason, it is important to support people who would not usually create knowledge to do so through their lenses on the world. That is the route to a more socially just world.

Ok, let's be honest, we said from the outset of this chapter that analysis often seemed the tricky part of the participatory research process. Some have gone so far to say that community members may find it tedious and time consuming, a struggle, not the best use of their time or entirely inaccessible (for example, if complex computer packages are used) (Warwick Booth, Bagnall and Coan, 2021: 110). However, we believe that, as one of the stages of research that most typically excludes co-researchers, it is especially important to make it inclusive and accessible to them. If you really can't find engaging ways to include the co-researchers, then we would say don't force it! If they are able to retain interest and power and agree to different ways of analysing data (such as you doing it as the participatory researcher or someone else being brought into help, such as the maths teacher from group A in our case studies) then this is far more important, as they are more likely to stay engaged for future parts of the process namely dissemination (discussed in Chapter 9) and getting their hard work out there for others to see.

Reflective task and tea break eight

- How often have you analysed data before?
- What did you think and feel about data analysis before reading this chapter?
- Have those thoughts and feelings changed at all?

- How do you think your co-researchers will respond to the idea of data analysis?
- How can you present the task to them in an appropriate and meaningful way?
- What will you do if they don't want to take part?

Summary

This chapter has described different types of data and different ways to analyse those data sets. The individual and subjective nature of data analysis has been stressed in order to reassure you that your process and findings will be right for you and the group. The chapter has encouraged you to support co-researchers to undertake analysis as this is an important step in knowledge generation.

Further reading

- There is an excellent chapter on participatory analysis in the following book: Warwick-Booth, L., Bagnall, A. and Coan, S. (2021) *Creating Participatory Research. Principles, Practice and Reality*, Bristol: Policy Press.
- This paper provides an example of participatory analysis: https://pubmed.ncbi.nlm.nih.gov/20208250/
- An accessible guide to statistics can be found here: Salkind, N. (2011) *Statistics for People Who Think they Hate Statistics* (4th edn), London: Sage.
- Further information on quantitative or statistical analysis: https://www.scribbr.com/statistics/descriptive-statistics/
- Here is an online guide to using excel for data analysis: https://www.youtube.com/watch?v=CnR3yDXZQ1M
- A good book on qualitative analysis can be found here: Saldana, J. (2009) *The Coding Manual for Qualitative Researchers*, London: Sage.
- Further information online on coding qualitative data: https://www.quirkos.com/blog/post/beginners-guide-coding-qualitative-data-analysis
- Further information on thematic analysis can be found in this link: https://www.youtube.com/watch?v=KUZ6iGvJlGI

- Further information on visual analysis is online here: https://www.matrix.edu.au/beginners-guide-year-9-english/part-7-how-analyse-images-visual-information/
- Information on the four data analysis software programmes we mentioned can be found at the following sites. A university partner might be able to share access to these with you, otherwise they can be expensive. Quirkos is the least expensive and most accessible:
  - Quirkos: https://www.quirkos.com/
  - Atlas.ti: https://atlasti.com/
  - NVIVO: https://www.qsrinternational.com/nvivo-qualitative-data-analysis-software/home
  - SPSS: https://www.ibm.com/uk-en/products/spss-statistics

9

How do we get our messages out there?

Chapter overview

This chapter will support you to identify the audience for your research, clarify the message you want them to hear and work out which kind of output they will be the most attentive to and how to get it to them. After working through these four processes you will have a dissemination strategy ready to roll out.

Who is your research audience?

So just who do you want to see, hear, use or learn from your research? The answer to this will largely depend on your research aim and you might have already thought this through – in fact, it's often a good idea to start with this in mind. If you have not identified an audience, then now is the time. Look back at your aim and work out who you want to share your research with in order to achieve that aim.

There is a huge range of potential audiences for your research and you might want to go back to your stakeholder map to see who you have already identified as interested and powerful in relation to your research. Figure 9.1 below might help you to identify further people who are important in your research.

Figure 9.1: Types of audiences

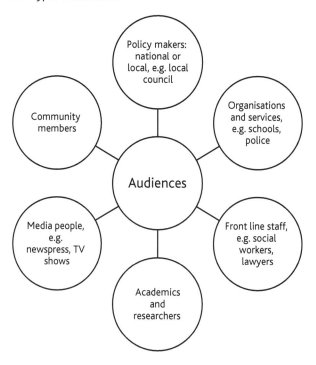

Going back to our case studies:

The students in group A wanted their school leaders to hear their research findings. Their fellow students were important stakeholders, but they were focused on influencing and making changes in school policy and so school leaders were their target audience.

The parents in group B wanted police and policymakers to hear their messages in order to achieve citywide change. If it was not possible to influence the police and policymakers themselves, they wanted as many people in the community to hear about the research so they might also apply pressure for change, so the general public were a potential audience.

The practitioners in group C wanted their individual and collective teams to hear the messages from the research as it progressed and once all the data had been collected so that they could all make changes to their practice – they were their own audience.

What is your message?

Having worked out who you want to influence with your research, you now need to work out what your message is. As you analyse your data you will develop a set of findings which you want people to see and act on. There might be a few findings and they could be varied. Your research message is the one single statement you want people to take away from your research. Imagine you only had 30 seconds of someone's time – what single thing would you say to them about your research? Your message is the overview of your research story.

Let's look to our case studies again to exemplify this:

The students' message was 'mental health in our school is worse than the national average in some domains – we need changes in our school policy'.

The parents' message was 'police stop and search policy is having a negative impact on whole families and communities – we need changes that include a community response within this policy'.

The practitioners' message was 'working more collectively and collaboratively, and less siloed, is more fulfilling and successful in our mission … here are some top tips to help us do it better'.

Your message might be clear from the outset; you may know what you want to communicate by looking at your aims. Sometimes, however, the message only emerges from the data. It is certainly worth checking at the end of the data analysis if the message is the same. This is the key thing you want everyone to know about what you did. Make sure you are all comfortable with sharing this message. If you have many different audiences you may also find you have a slightly different message for each one. You can map these out in the dissemination strategy.

Which outputs will be the most effective?

Now you know who you want to talk to and what you want them to hear. The next question is what they will be most likely to pay attention to. This means you need to work out the preferences of the group of people you are talking to. Some audiences will prefer formal outputs such as reports – governments, professional bodies and organisations are likely to prefer these. This is not the case for everyone though. Some people, for example younger people, may prefer more informal outputs such as a film. If you want to reach a range of people all at once you might want to put on a performance.

In our case studies:

The group of students wrote a report, making sure it was full of bright and eye-catching infographics representing their numerical findings. They thought a short and impactful report would be more likely to influence their school leaders.

The group of parents created an audio-visual presentation of the key themes and suggestions from the research that they wanted to present to key stakeholders. Within this presentation they referred to short films that narrated the stories that came out of the research. These were posted across social media for a community-wide message (see the last section of this chapter).

The group of practitioners wrote a digital 'playbook' – a 'how to' guide to collaborative working, with a set of core principles for all to sign up to and check in on. These principles were also printed as posters and put on office walls.

It is useful to name an output for each audience and state why you think that is the right output for that group. You may find that there are a few assumptions – which may or may not be correct. The important thing is that all the co-researchers sign up to the decision as to what to create and that they have the skills and resources to produce that particular output.

Reports

Reports often seem the simplest way to convey your research findings. However, writing a report demands that you present your findings in a linear and logical order which may not fully reflect their complexity. Reports tend to use formal language which can remove the feelings of the research and the sense of the researchers. This may be useful in very sensitive subjects but might flatten out important richness. Whilst reports are easy to print, hand out or email, they may not be accessible to everyone. People with low levels of literacy may not be able to write or read a report. Time can be another challenge, and busy policymakers may not want to read all the details you have to present. Adding summaries and infographics can overcome this challenge to some extent.

Posters and infographics

One way to overcome the 'flat' structure of a report is to add images and infographics. An infographic is an image that conveys a research finding – it could be a chart or graph, or some icons that creatively convey meaning. These can engage a reader more readily than lengthy text, but you are also less sure of the audience fully understanding the context of the finding. Sometimes infographics can stand alone as posters, which may be useful to get your work out there, or sometimes they can add to a written piece. Access to an artist or desktop publishing software might be a limitation of this approach.

Presentation formats

Presentations allow the audience to see and hear from the researchers directly and can be a more compelling way of conveying research findings and a richer story to be told. Presentations could be delivered live, pre-recorded or both.

Findings could be presented in a classical seminar/webinar style and could be filmed. Alternatively, if the researchers do not want to be featured, you could create a video of images with a voice-over or narrate over a PowerPoint presentation. These many options provide flexibility in how you can create presentations and in how people access them. It may be difficult to get an audience together to watch your findings in person, and many researchers and co-researchers find delivering presentations challenging and so these limitations also need consideration. Outweighing these limitations could be the reach achieved by posting a short film on social media.

Performances

Another option is to create a performance to convey your findings. This could be a piece of theatre, a puppet show, a dance or something musical. Performances are best suited to conveying the emotion of a piece of research. They can also be combined with presentations to give a rounded experience of the findings. A challenge to disseminating in this style might be the confidence and skills of the team to perform and the time needed to rehearse.

Websites

A website could be another way to share your findings with the general public. They are not very useful if you have a small group of people you want to influence, but they are very visual and dynamic and allow a lot of freedom in how findings are presented. The greatest disadvantage are the technical skills, connectivity and funds needed to set up some online presence.

Gallery or installation

Visual research lends itself well to the creation of a gallery or art installation. This could be of artefacts or artworks created in the research process or created afterwards specifically to convey the research. There could be explanations of the artworks or they could be left to speak for themselves. Video and audio clips could also be part of an installation. A key question here is about the physical space, costs for using it and how key stakeholders or the wider public might access it.

Publication

The research team might also decide they want to get their research into print. There are three choices here – to produce a story that will sell into local or national newspapers, to write a piece for a professional magazine/website or to publish in an academic journal. Getting into print might give the work more credibility and might help the right audience access it. Academic journals can be a challenge to publish in, however, some, such as the Social Publishing Foundation, are committed to supporting all participatory research groups to successfully publish in their online knowledge base.

You will notice throughout this that you are continually balancing two demands – the first is to meet the needs of the audience, to communicate with them in ways that will engage and convince them. The second demand, but equally as important, is that you need to use a style of communication that all the research team are confident in and able to access.

No matter which type of output you use, you will probably need to say similar things. Usually research outputs include the following:

- Introduction and context: why this research is going on; what else was happening at the same time; what was the starting point for it.
- Approach: how did you go about the research. This section will include everything you have planned so far, the aims, questions, methods, data collection tools, participants and so on.
- Findings: this is where you would report what has been found through the research.
- Conclusion and recommendations: what you want people to think and do as a result of your research.

Great news – you've probably already planned or even written part of the final output, just by reading this book and adopting its structure! You might not use such formal headings for all outputs, they wouldn't work well in a performance for example, but you might use them as a 'storyline' in your performance or video.

What is the best way to communicate your message?

The final decision in the dissemination chain involved the communication channel. Again, this decision is based on your knowledge of or assumptions about the audience. It may be that a written letter and hard copy report will get read, or perhaps an email and electronic report is more likely to be opened. For local impact, face-to-face meetings or phone calls may work best. And, for anything with extensive reach, social media might be the tool of choice. You may need a mix of communication channels to ensure as much reach as possible or to cater to a range of audiences too.

Planning your dissemination strategy to achieve social justice

Most participatory research projects focus on achieving some kind of social change – that is one of the ways in which they contribute to social justice. It is also likely that your project has aimed to be meaningful and impactful for the co-researchers involved. This is most likely to be the case if change happens as a result of their efforts – that would encourage them to further engage in research for change.

Working out an effective dissemination strategy, using the template in Table 9.1 is really important to give yourselves the best chance of influencing your audiences to make changes that will lead to the positive impact you ultimately aim for.

What if it doesn't work?

Things don't always go well and sometimes our best attempts to create impact fall short. One example of this is from Central University, New York. A community-based participatory project (The Morris Justice Project) researched levels of stop and search in New York and the number of weapons found in

Table 9.1: An example of a dissemination strategy

Audience	Research message	Research output	Communication channel

the process. (You'll see here the project that one of our fictional case studies was based on.) More Black youth were stopped than White youth, and yet they had less weapons than the White youth – a clear injustice. The team tried to communicate this to the New York Police Department but they did not want to read their report. Instead, the team hired a huge lorry-mounted projector and loud speakers and did a live public dissemination event in downtown New York, projecting their findings onto the side of a skyscraper.

Now that got their attention!

You may not need to turn to such drastic measures, but it is useful to note the determination and creativity you may need in order to get your research in front of the right people.

This example does also bring our attention back to the ethical issues inherent in participatory research (discussed in Chapter 10). Some forms of dissemination may intentionally reveal the identity of the co-researchers in order to give them credit for their work. This may, however, place them at risk from stakeholders who do not agree with the way the research was done or what it has shown. The risks of identification of authorship through dissemination therefore needs careful consideration and agreement.

Reflective task and tea break nine

Think about how you will develop a dissemination plan with the co-researchers:

• What do they need to know to be able to do this?
• What process will allow everyone to have an equal say?
• How will you decide who will do what?

- How can you share tasks equitably?
- What impact would it have if no one listened?

Summary

This chapter has introduced four different but linked aspects of a dissemination strategy; working out who your audience are, what the research message is, what the most appropriate research output is and how to communicate it. The chapter has positioned dissemination as an important link in the chain that leads to positive impact.

Further reading

- This guide provides more details on dissemination: The Community Alliance for Research and Engagement (2021) 'Beyond scientific publication: strategies for disseminating research findings', Available at: https://www.idaea.csic.es/sites/default/files/CARE-Beyond-Scientific-Publication-Strategies-for-Disseminating-Research-Findings.pdf
- The Morris Justice Project is the research we loosely based case study B on, you can find out more about it here: https://morrisjustice.org/
- Research Retold provides an overview of four creative forms of dissemination: https://www.researchretold.com/creative-methods-of-research-dissemination/#:~:text=Over all%2C%20performative%20arts%2C%20participatory%20fil mmaking,truly%20bring%20research%20to%20life
- This Public Health Centre Research Information Service video gives a good overview of dissemination strategies: https://www.youtube.com/watch?v=TES_cB4pKGw
- The Social Publishing Foundation support all participatory researchers to publish their work free of charge on their open access knowledge base. You can find out more here: https://www.socialpublishersfoundation.org/
- A detailed dissemination plan template is available here: https://guides.library.vcu.edu/c.php?g=480243&p=6785181
- This text provides a good overview of participatory research and has a great chapter discussing participatory dissemination: Warwick-Booth, L., Bagnall, A. and Coan, S. (2021) *Creating Participatory Research – Principles, Practice and Reality*, Bristol: Policy Press.
- Whilst not purely participatory, this text presents excellent innovative ideas for dissemination: Jungnickel, K. (2020) *Transmissions: Critical Tactics for Making and Communicating Research*, Cambridge, MA, MIT Press.

10

How do we keep everyone safe?

Chapter overview

This chapter will provide an overview of how to keep participants and co-researchers as safe as possible through 'research ethics'. The principles and practicalities of different ethical considerations will be discussed and the particular challenges of participatory research raised.

What are research ethics?

Research ethics are a set of principles that have been developed to keep researchers and the people they research safe – physically, mentally and emotionally. We take many principles for granted nowadays, but they have developed from examples of unethical research in the past. We would never now think of stealing data, but many First Nations communities have had their data stolen without their consent in the past. We would think it terrible to deceive participants in a study, but that did happen in the past in some experiments on human behaviour. Thankfully, as a result of these, we now have a better understanding of and a commitment to ethical research.

Research ethics are often written as sets of statements or principles and the task in research design is to ensure that they can all be met within the research project before it commences. The process is rather like a risk assessment, with the researchers thinking through the risks posed under each ethical principle and how to avoid or limit risk and damage. Sometimes someone in an organisation will approve the ethical plans before the work can start. This would be the case for research led by a university or a health care trust. Some sectors do not have their own ethical committee but may still have research ethics, for example there is a set of educational research ethics in Britain to guide research design in schools, but no central ethical approval system for teachers. Whether you need ethical approval or not, you still need to identify and manage as many ethical issues as possible before the project commences. In a participatory project this would be done with the co-researchers as part of the co-design process.

One of the difficulties of participatory research is its organic developmental nature. The researchers may not know the exact terms of the project before working with the co-researchers. This can make it difficult to get ethical approval from an institutional board before the participatory research project commences and so a staged process might be needed, as we describe below. Some ethical panels may not be experienced in the many nuances of participatory research and therefore feel more inclined to deny ethical approval, and this has created a barrier for many academics wanting to work in a meaningful way with communities. We have found that working with ethical panels openly and offering them training in participatory methods enables such difficulties to be resolved.

A two-stage process in participatory ethics

We suggest a two-stage process as both good practice in participatory research as well as for formal ethical applications. The first stage involves outlining plans to engage with a group of co-researchers to design and carry out a research project, no matter which of the three origins of the participatory research:

1. You go to members of a group or community wanting to do some research with them.
2. Members of a group or community come to you wanting to do some research with you.
3. You decide to do some research together as you are engaged with other activities with the group or community.

This will ensure the way you set up the project with the co-researchers is ethical. The second stage of ethics is for the co-researchers to discuss any ethical issues in the research you intend to co-design and carry out together. Having been through it once in the first stage, you might have learnt about how you can support the ethical process with co-researchers.

Each of our case studies involved a slightly different approach.

For group A, where the participatory researchers approached the students, ethics were first considered in engaging co-researchers before the students or school had been identified. Ethical approval was gained from the university ethics panel where the participatory researchers were based. This was particularly significant as the students were likely to be under 18. They then ran an ethics training session with the students and co-created the ethics for working with the research participants. This was taken back to the university ethics panel, as had been agreed in the first stage of ethical approval.

For group B, where the group of parents approached the participatory researchers, a similar ethics session was run, but this was more co-developed and considered first 'how we'll work safely together as (a) co-researchers, and (b) as participants' and then 'how we'll work safely with others'. This was jointly submitted to a university ethics board very early in the group's formation.

For group C, where the group of practitioners and trainers decided to research together, they again co-developed ethics, running through the process together but focusing on the participants within their teams. No formal ethical permission was gained from a university.

Ongoing ethics

Whilst planning for ethical research happens at the outset, managing ethics is an ongoing process. Issues will arise throughout the project as it develops and so revisiting, discussing and amending plans to manage ethical issues needs to happen continually. People's roles might change during the research causing issues, participants might get upset and need support and accidents may happen, such as data being lost. Issues like these may not all be anticipated at the outset. This is sometimes called '**running ethics**' to show it's a dynamic process throughout the whole project. This is particularly important in a participatory project as outlined in each of the principles below.

Transparency

One key principle is to ensure everyone involved in the research knows everything they need to know about the research so they can make an informed decision as to whether to take part or not. This means providing a summary of the project to co-researchers and participants, often called a '**participant information form**'. This details what the research is about, why they have been asked to participate, what it will involve, any benefits to the participants, how the data will be used and where the findings will be published. This will need to be produced in a format that is accessible and meaningful to the participants. There is a risk that presenting too much formal information too early could deter participants from getting involved. But they do need to fully understand what they are getting involved in. Alternatives to written information could include workshops, videos and one-to-one conversations.

One of the challenges of engaging co-researchers in a participatory study is that you do not know exactly how the project will unfold over time. You do not even know the research question. Whilst you can be transparent about this, it is challenging to recruit people to work with you when you don't know what it will involve. This highlights the importance of ongoing communication and ethical discussions at each step of the research process.

A perfect example of this can be found in group A from our case studies, where the participatory researchers had no idea what approach the co-researchers would want to take in the research. None of the methods, sample or data collection tools were known at this point so they couldn't gain ethical consent for them within their initial application. The co-researchers wanted to use surveys which made the next stage of the ethics approval somewhat easier, as the students would not be directly talking to other students on the sensitive subject of their mental health and because all of the data collection would be anonymous from the outset (discussed further below).

Consent and withdrawal

Once participants are clear about the research and their involvement in it, they are in a position to give their '**informed consent**' to take part. This usually takes the form of participants signing a statement to say they understand the project and what they are choosing to undertake. This enables any future complaints about the research to be traced back and any participants to be contactable. The researchers are responsible for keeping a list of all the consents and participant details to make this possible.

Several issues may arise from this. Many of the participants we seek to work with may not want to or be able to sign a written document. Alternative formats for giving consent may therefore need to be found such as an audio recording, a poster with signatures or a photograph of someone holding a statement.

A second issue is someone's capacity to give consent for themselves. People with intellectual disabilities, cognitive impairment or who are of a young age may not understand what is being asked of them and are therefore unable to give consent. Many organisations will always seek a parent or carer's consent for children under the age of 16 to safeguard against young people taking part in projects they do not fully understand.

Similarly, parents and carers could give consent for someone with an intellectual disability or cognitive impairment. Whether it is appropriate for them to be involved in the research if they are unable to consent for themselves is another issue to consider. If your research involves members of staff in an organisation you may also need to gain organisational consent before approaching them, creating another layer of consent. This was certainly a consideration within the case study of group C as the practitioners were working with multi-agency teams and thus multiple organisational consent was needed.

It is important to remind ourselves of the participatory values and issues of power at this point. Even when we think additional consent is needed, we still need to gain the co-researcher or participants' consent. Otherwise, we could end up in a situation where they don't feel empowered, feel powerless or are completely disempowered (for example, if a carer gives consent but the participant doesn't).

In many research projects, consent is an individual affair as data is often collected from individuals. With a participatory project, however, collective consent might also be necessary. Working together as co-researchers in your own community may need permission from all key stakeholders, or even all community members. Working together in a research project may reveal information about people that co-researchers live and work with, and so collective consent should also be considered (Flicker et al., 2007).

This was exemplified with group B from our case studies, where consideration needed to be given to the children and family members that the parents were interviewing each other about. The team had to decide whether consent needed to be gained from children and families if their experiences were being discussed.

Consent is often dealt with at the start of a research project on the assumption that it may only involve a single, simple, data collection point, such as an interview. If, however, a project is complex, multi-method or participatory, people may be asked to do several things and the project might evolve over time. In these instances, just as we discussed above with ongoing ethics, it is therefore more appropriate to ask for consent step by step so people understand each part of the process.

The key question, therefore, is who needs to give consent, on what basis and how often.

Rights to withdraw consent

Allied to volunteering to participate and giving informed consent is the right to withdraw from research. At any point any participant should be able to withdraw. This is also part of the information they need at the start of the project, which includes who they need to contact, how and how will their data be removed from the research. If there is a point in the research where this is impossible (for example, after publication) they should be notified of this too.

Anonymity and confidentiality

It is generally taken for granted that someone who participates in research should have a right to anonymity. This means that data is anonymised and any findings are shown without a name or anything else that could identify them. Keeping someone's identity confidential can be problematic. In some small communities someone may be identifiable by their gender, age and job. Researchers should therefore also consider what details need to be removed from the data, beyond just names, in order to ensure identities remain confidential (for example, voice, visual or circumstantial). This may even take the form of changing some demographic details to obscure an identity, as long as it would not compromise the meaning of the data itself.

This is much harder in participatory research because the co-researchers know one another as they work together on the research and they may well know the people they conduct research with. Whilst names and identities can be removed from any research outputs or published documents, the co-researchers cannot 'unlearn' what they discovered about community members or one another in the research. This was a consideration for both groups B and C from our case studies. This must be fully discussed as part of the transparency of the research, and individual and collective consent given in light of some of the implications discussed below.

A final complication of participatory research is the naming of co-researchers themselves. All participatory research projects wish to give acknowledgement equally to the work of the entire research team. This would mean naming the co-researchers in any research outputs, which then makes them fully identifiable. Many institutional research ethics boards will not allow this, but acknowledgement might be really meaningful to the co-researchers. Discussing the possibilities of attribution at the start of a project is therefore important in order to enable it to happen where desirable or to manage expectations where it is not possible.

In the case studies, group A were all named as co-researchers – there were only positives to be gained from them being acknowledged. However, in both groups B and C the co-researchers decided collectively their individual names should not be used. For group B they were referred to as 'members of the community' and for group C they were referred to as 'multi-agency teams'.

Protection from harm

Protecting participants and researchers from harm is another common sense and laudable principle. At its most tangible this would mean that medical research would not place a participant at a health risk. For social research the risks to participants are usually emotional or interpersonal. For example, discussing a sensitive topic may be distressing. Researchers need to make sure they reduce the possibility for distress, disclose the possibility for distress and have procedures in place for if participants do become distressed. Again, this is at two levels – co-researchers may become distressed in hearing or learning things through the research and participants may become distressed in sharing those things.

Physical risks from social research are also possible. If we consider an investigation into gang involvement, being seen to participate may identify someone as gang involved, placing them at physical risk from other gangs or judicial risk from the police. This was certainly a consideration for the parents in case study B.

Interpersonal issues may also arise from participation in research, particularly in community-based research projects where co-researchers may be perceived as becoming more powerful than other community members. This could cause resentment or conflict.

The same issues stand for the researcher. Whilst physical safety travelling to perhaps remote research sites needs consideration, so too does the impact of listening to distressing stories and being seen as a researcher or 'nosy person' in a community.

Whilst protection from risk and harm remains a clear principle in research, the complications of participatory and community-based research mean it may not be guaranteed. Some reassurances can be found however from Lundy and McGovern (2006: 62) who found that:

> the best means of dealing with the ethical problems of sensitivity and danger was to ensure that those taking part understood precisely what the project was for, felt a sense of ownership and agency over its outcomes and could directly shape and control their deeply personal and often emotionally difficult involvement in it.

In other words, the participatory process (democratic dialogue) is the key way to overcome the issues participatory research itself creates.

Safeguarding

'**Safeguarding**' is the term commonly used to describe how we keep people safe, particularly if they '**disclose**' they are at risk of harm or have caused harm to others. It refers predominantly to young people but is also applicable to adults. In effect, it means that when explaining how you will work with the participants you can promise to keep their data confidential but you will be unable to keep any issue of safeguarding confidential. Such disclosures would need to be passed on to other authorities, such as a social worker or the police. It will be important for you to understand any such safeguarding procedures in your country and what you may or may not be able to promise to keep confidential. This obviously will need special attention, and potentially specific training, when working with co-researchers to help them know what to do in the event that something is disclosed to them.

Research roles

Usually the role of the researcher and the participant are very clear cut and also very hierarchical. The researcher controls the research, asks the questions, writes up the data and publishes the work, and the participant simply provides data. However, in participatory research the roles are much more blurred. You, as the participatory researcher, may find yourself working as a facilitator, community organiser, popular educator, researcher and activist in a short space of time. The co-researchers could find themselves in multiple roles, potentially engaged in every stage of the research process as co-researchers, and maybe as participants contributing data too. This is a further complication ethically as roles are more fluid than in traditional research.

For group B, the parents were both the researchers asking questions and the participants answering questions. For group C, the practitioners were initially delegates/trainees on a training programme, then co-researchers, then facilitators in their own teams' developmental journey.

Therefore, an important ethical dimension in participatory research is to ensure that the research team is equipped with the skills and knowledge to undertake any activity and role, and that the cost of doing so (economic, emotional or relational) is not too great. Building time into participation projects for learning skills together is an important ethical dimension.

Incentives, remuneration and benefits to participants

It is useful to identify at the outset any benefit that the participants may gain from taking part in the project. This may involve telling their story, being listened to, being able to influence research, gaining skills and much more. This is part of transparency and letting people know how they might gain and a form of reciprocity.

Many research traditions consider incentives as inappropriate in a research setting. Their fear is that offering an incentive would make someone participate who would not otherwise do so, or in a way they would not normally, and in so doing will bias the research. For example, they may say something to please the researcher that they would not normally say.

An alternative view is that incentives offer some remuneration for participation and, whilst typically small, are very fair. The National Institute for Health Research (2021) in the UK now recommends a remuneration of at least travel expenses and the provision of refreshments at events, and the consideration of other appropriate forms of payment. For many participants a token, gift voucher or cash payment does recompense their efforts in giving data. This is also an acknowledgement of power, and particularly the participant's knowledge as valuable and of worth (in terms of acknowledgement, remuneration or other).

When working over an extended period of time with co-researchers, the issue of remuneration becomes even more important. Participatory researchers are likely to be receiving a salary for their work in the project, or it may be part of their own studies or professional development or they are gaining in some other way. In the interests of equity, so should the co-researchers. But how much they can be paid is a difficult question. Some people struggle to find the time to support the research, and in doing so they may lose the opportunity to earn money elsewhere, so it is sometimes a vital component of participation. Some funders or organisations will not pay for co-researchers' time or offer incentives. Seeing community members receiving payment for their research work may also create additional interpersonal issues and competition for co-research roles and so the issue needs careful consideration and discussion in the community.

Data protection

Data protection refers to what data you have a right to request, how data will be collected, how you will store data and for how long. Many countries have regulations on what data can be collected about individuals. At the very least, they require us to commit to only collecting data which is useful and letting participants know how that data will be used. This means that designing the data collection tools has an ethical dimension too, such as only asking questions where the answers are absolutely necessary to the project.

Data can be recorded in a variety of ways – in notes, photographs, drawings, documents, audio recordings and video recordings. Participants should be informed of how their data will be captured and asked specifically to consent to that form of capture.

Once captured, data will need to be securely stored. If it is physical data, plans need to be made for where it can be physically locked. If it is electronic data, its location and cybersecurity will need to be considered. Aligned to this practical concern is who then has access to the data and ownership of it. This would usually be the researcher but this may not be the case in participatory research.

Participants should also be informed of how long their data will be stored and how it will be destroyed. Who has responsibility for this in participatory research is another key question as it is likely to be a date after the completion of the project.

In addition to the participatory angle raised on ethics in each section above, there are some particular ethical challenges to working in participatory research.

Partnership and power

We have alluded to the importance of power sharing throughout this chapter as it is so fundamental to participatory research. Yet it may not be as simple to undertake as it first seems. Partnerships need careful and open negotiation if agendas are to be reconciled, and collaboration has to be deliberately developed rather than being left to chance. The team can engage in reflexive practice throughout to help this. This seeks to realise and discuss who has power, how it manifests and what impact that has on the project. Participatory work has a commitment to this rich but sometimes uncomfortable terrain.

Researchers have traditionally held power in research projects. Participatory research rejects this, which creates additional tensions as made explicit in the section on roles. This also poses challenges for different stages of the research process. For example, data is traditionally owned and stored by a researcher and outputs are published by the researcher. It may also be easy for researchers to unconsciously start to take control of the process in their efforts to support the project, turning what was participative into something co-opted.

Consideration of who owns what and who can share what is vital in a participatory project. This is particularly tricky in situations such as group C, where there are multiple sources of data coming together. There is no clear map of what might be 'right' or 'wrong' in any given context. Some participants may need support in saying 'no' to researchers or other group members who have strong views. Finding ways to make this possible is a small but significant aspect of the teamwork.

Community rights and conflict

We have touched on some of the challenges from having a privileged co-researcher position in communities – with additional influence, knowledge and perhaps also payment. Added to this is the difficulty of 'community' as a term. A community can be defined by place, interest and commonality, and every community has a boundary for inclusion or exclusion. This can be challenging to manage in a process dedicated to democracy. There may be tensions between community groups and difficulty in deciding who gets to represent which community. Community relations and group dynamics need careful management.

Social justice and action

Participatory research has a commitment to bringing about actions for social change as a result of the research process. What counts as action, who undertakes those actions and what changes are sought will also need careful negotiation. These might be very different for the stakeholders and might have very different implications for them. For example, in countries where freedom of speech is limited, it may be too risky to undertake activism. The action orientation of participatory research is challenging, and the actions that might be needed are not visible from the starting point so it is difficult to know who will be able to commit to them. Indeed, one of the strongest critiques of participatory research is the lack of evidence of it effecting social change despite its laudable aims (Schubotz, 2019). There is much evidence of its benefits to co-researchers and participants (which arguably also benefit society) but very little on social change itself arising directly from research projects of this type.

Effecting positive change is also a key concern ethically. Groups and communities may need to consider whether the research findings will promote positive social change or further reinforce stigma, marginalisation and stereotypes in society.

Given how many times we have referred to discussion with the co-researchers, stakeholders and community, it is perhaps no surprise that we advocate for what Banks and Brydon-Miller (2018: 11) call 'communitarian ethics'. This approach to ethics is rooted in the real-world realities of each situation or context rather than abstract principles and regard ethics as a way of being, as well as a way of doing research.

Reflective task and tea break ten

- How will you present the different ethical principles to the co-researchers?
- What activity could you engage in with them to decide how to tackle each one?

Summary

This chapter has introduced you to the principles and practices of ethical research as a field, and of participatory research in particular. Fundamental to ethics in participatory research is discussion and dialogue on a continual basis. This is only possible in well founded, mutually respectful and trusting relationships which are the bedrock of participation.

Further reading

- This paper unpacks some of the ethics inherent in socially just research: DePalma, R. (2010) 'Socially just research for social justice: negotiating consent and safety in a participatory action research project', *International Journal of Research and Method in Education*, 33(3): 215–27. Available at: https://www.researchgate.net/publication/233076659_Socially_just_research_for_social_justice_Negotiating_consent_and_safety_in_a_participatory_action_research_project

- Sarah and Mary's book is a wonderful guide to participatory ethics in all settings, but particularly health and social wellbeing research, with theory, practical tips and rich case studies: Banks, S. and Brydon-Miller, M. (2018) *Ethics in Participatory Research for Health and Wellbeing*, Abingdon: Routledge.

- The Connected Communities initiative have a guide that thoroughly explores the complexities of collaborative and co-produced research relationships: Facer, K. and Enright, B. (2016) *Creating Living Knowledge*, Bristol: University of Bristol, Available at: https://research-information.bris.ac.uk/ws/portalfiles/portal/75082783/FINAL_FINAL_CC_Creating_Living_Knowledge_Report.pdf

- A universalist approach to ethics is adopted in social sciences in the UK and can be accessed here: www.acass.org.uk

11

Doing and reviewing participatory research

Chapter overview

This chapter will talk through how to 'get on with it'! That is how to do your research project having planned it all out in a participatory manner with the help of the first ten chapters. We will discuss how you move from research design planning to project planning as well as covering teamwork and problem solving as keys to successful implementation. We also talk about the 'messiness' you are likely to encounter in research in order to reassure you this is okay. The final half of this chapter goes on to discuss how you can review and evaluate quality and success with co-researchers throughout the process, as well as at the end.

Project planning: how to plan what will happen when

From our perspective, as long as we've sorted our ethics, let's just get on with it! You'll most certainly learn as you go and tweak the project with the co-researchers. Acceptance of this evolving approach helps you jump in. This seems especially important as the early part of 'doing' is likely to be delivery planning which seems like not doing! But you'll be doing this with the co-researchers and so it is most certainly 'doing'.

By working through the chapters in this book you will have developed a good understanding of research design and how to undertake a project with co-researchers. You may still need to collectively decide what order things will happen in, who will do them, when they need to be done by and how you will know they have been completed. Collaborative project planning is helpful here – it enables you to turn your research design into a project plan for everyone to work from.

In group A from our case studies, the project plan had to take account of students' school timetables and ensure it fitted into a regular weekly timetabled slot. This provided a helpful overall structure and parameters to work within. It never appeared to be restricting, perhaps because this was what the students were used to, and perhaps because they shaped their project to fit within this as they knew their boundaries.

In group B the project plan needed to be much more fluid to meet the different schedules of group members, as well as to access further participants.

In group C the planning was all done digitally on an online project board to help with the dispersed geographical spread and to keep momentum and communication up between face-to-face sessions.

There are lots of templates you can download from the internet to help you with project planning, but a simple table, drawn on a large sheet of paper or in an online document, can also work just fine. These are the things we believe you should consider including:

1. Activities – what are all the different research activities that you've considered and what order do they need to happen in? Try to put them in some sort of sequence, even if they overlap.

2. Where – jot down where each activity will take place: a room, address or online platform.
3. Who needs to be there – identify all the people needed to make that activity a success.
4. Who is leading – who will volunteer to manage that particular activity, making sure it happens.
5. Resources – what do you need to make the activity a success? Is it money, stationary, food and drink? What has to be there to make it a success?
6. Start date – when will work on this activity start?
7. End date – when will this activity be completed?
8. Milestones – what are the key indicators that will show success along the way? What will have been done, what will you have to show for it?
9. Risk – is there anything that would threaten the success of the activity and how can you overcome that risk?

You will have already thought through the detail of what will happen with your research design; now you add the detail of where, when and who. Those headings create a table like Table 11.1 which you might find useful.

Chapter activity

You might want to pause right now for a tea break and sit down with your favourite brew and work through this table with a project you have done in the past or have in mind for the future.

Table 11.1: Project plan template

Activity	Where	When	Who's there	Who leads	Resources	Start date	End date	Milestones	Risk

You can design your own template of course or work out a plan in an entirely different way. Each of the activity leaders might then want to develop a more detailed plan of how they will make their activity happen, talking to the people leading the activities before and after to ensure everything fits together.

It's a messy business: expect mess and challenges

Mess might arise because you and the co-researchers are human beings with many other things going on in your lives: other work, caring responsibilities, illness and other significant life events might disrupt your beautifully laid plans. That does not mean your planning was wrong, just that plans change.

Mess might also arrive because some of the planned research activities are suddenly impossible. Perhaps an organisation you wanted to work with closes down, maybe a community is distracted by another issue, perhaps no one wants to talk to you and maybe even a pandemic! These are all well-known issues that can crop up in the research. This does not mean you had a bad research design, just that research is sometimes complicated and unpredictable.

Every single one of our case studies had to cope with mess or change. Most notably co-researchers dropping out and in one case – group C – a whole team dropping out as their service was shut down.

Mess is also fairly inevitable in the kind of research you are doing – participatory research. A wonderful colleague, Tina Cook, put it like this:

> Engaging in action research, research that can disturb both individual and communally held notions of knowledge for practice, will be messy. Investigations into the 'messy area', the interface between the known and the nearly known, between knowledge-in-use and tacit knowledge as yet to be useful, reveal the 'messy area' as a vital element for seeing, disrupting, analysing, learning, knowing and changing. It is the place where long-held views shaped by professional knowledge,

practical judgement, experience and intuition are seen through other lenses. It is here that reframing takes place and new knowing, that has both theoretical and practical significance, arises: a 'messy turn' takes place. (Cook, 2009)

You are likely to be researching a complex question or issue with a group of people who will have similarities and differences. This is bound to create exciting new, but also 'messy', results. Remember, finding lots of different views, themes and ideas is a sign of good quality participatory research.

Teamwork: how will we work together and who will do what

It now becomes clear that, whilst there might be times when everyone works together, there may also be times when the co-researchers work in smaller groups or even solo. Hopefully, having planned all the research together, you are now feeling like a team of co-researchers, but teamwork sometimes takes time and effort to achieve.

We're going to assume that most people reading this book are experienced in this area from your own practice – this is a 'practitioner guide' after all. However, some people may not be, and so we make no apology for stating what some might say is the obvious!

The benefit of teamwork is the range of skills, knowledge, experience and networks that different people bring into the team. These hopefully complement one another, allowing the team to achieve more together than the individuals would alone. We think it is always helpful to acknowledge and celebrate individual contributions, to make them visible to the whole team. It will also show any gaps! Another practical consideration is that a team can divide a large and overwhelming task up into smaller more manageable tasks. Ideally these would be suited to each individual, but such a perfect fit may not be possible.

The reality of teamwork can be different to this. Whilst mild respectful disagreements can be productive, forceful personality differences that lead to disruptive conflicts can undermine team performance. The opposite effect is groupthink, in which team members all too quietly accept initial ideas without sufficient spirited discussion of alternatives. Teams also face difficulties when one or more team members don't contribute as much as others expect or people are jealous of the activities other people are undertaking compared to their own.

This was particularly challenging for group C from our case studies, with the geographical spread, and is precisely why they employed a digital workspace to help with connection, communication and momentum.

Some tensions and disagreements are inevitable. In families, friendships, social groups and teams there are always moments of discord. The trick, perhaps, is to 'manage' these well, so that they don't escalate into something more dramatic. The term 'manage' seems a little jarring in this book and so to qualify this, we mean to support or facilitate. And to qualify this further – this may not be you as the participatory researcher! It could be someone else in the group that has the experience or qualities.

Developing open and trusting relationships is key to this. Team members need to be able to speak freely but respectfully to one another and to be able to give and receive feedback. This is why participatory research (and teamwork) is often time intensive. Developing these relationships of mutual respect and trust, where anything can be aired, takes time.

Other practical ways to avoid tensions are:

- Make goals and plans clear so everyone knows what they are doing and how their activities fit into the whole plan.
- Make expectations and boundaries clear so people know when they are doing well.
- Review progress regularly and discuss issues early and openly.
- Celebrate everyone's success – celebrate what they do (effort) as well as what they achieve (outcomes).

We have come from backgrounds in social and educational research, practice, leadership and training and development. For us, there is a common thread running through all of these activities of a facilitative coaching approach. This is especially relevant when working in a participatory way and involves the core components of listening, empathy and being non-judgmental. The importance of this type of relationship is vital and worth working hard on to ensure mutual respect, rapport, role modelling desired behaviours and the permission to challenge undesirable behaviours. This is an empowering approach, with shared power and belief in the group to be able to come together to solve problems.

Problem solving: dealing with delays and issues

Despite our reassurances that it's okay for things to get a bit tense, late, change or be messy, it can still feel a blow when these problems arise. So, how can you support the group in learning to deal with them?

We advocate a solution-focused approach. Although it originated as a therapy model, this approach is now being applied with great success to coaching and team and organisational change. There are three principles within it that are strongly aligned with participatory research. These are:

- Focus on solutions not problems. You get what you focus on! Focusing on the problem won't necessarily help you reach the solution – the more time spent talking about the problem is time you're not moving towards the solution. You can help this by steering the conversation forwards to where you are trying to get to and asking things like 'so what are our options here?'
- People already have the resources they need to change. You and the co-researchers will have the answers, or the capacity to find the answers, but it might take some time and reflection to find them.
- Change happens in small steps. And a small change can have big consequences – so start with just a tiny tweak and you might find that unlocks answers to the bigger problems you were facing.

Here are some tools that people use to keep a focus on solutions and to unlock knowledge.

1. Wild ideas

What are all the ideas we can come up with here, from the sensible to the ludicrous; from the small to the massive – what are all the different ways we could solve or reduce this problem?

2. The 'miracle question'

This question helps you focus on the solution without worrying about how 'realistic' it is or how to get there.

> Imagine that while you're asleep tonight a miracle happens and the problem is completely solved. You don't realise this, of course, because you're still asleep – so when you wake up what will be the first thing that tells you that this miracle has happened? What else will tell you (get as much detail as you can)?

3. Appreciative Inquiry

'When/where/what is working – even just a bit?' 'What's helping that?'
'When has it worked elsewhere, or in the past?' 'What's helped that?'
'What have you been doing well that's stopped the situation from getting worse?'

4. Scaling

Scaling is another way to find the seeds of the solution in the current situation, and also to help bridge the apparent gap between the present and the future solution.

- On a scale of 1–10, where 1 is the worst it's ever been, and 10 is how you're going to be when you've sorted the problem out completely, what number are you at now?
- How did you get from n-1 to n?
- What will be different when you are at n+1?

These are all tried and tested ways for teams to identify their own solutions to their own problems – we hope you enjoy playing with them.

Evaluating success and identifying learning: process and outcome

It's likely that you have been reflecting on each stage of the research as you have been planning and thinking about it. It's also important to do this as you are undertaking it. Regular 'check ins' or reflective reviews at the end of each meeting with co-researchers is often invaluable.

In our case studies, this was scheduled with group A as part of the weekly sessions and because of the fit with timetabling. This resulted in a structured weekly routine.

If you and the team are used to reflecting throughout the process it is likely they are working better together, learning more as they go, solving problems more quickly and will find evaluating the project even easier. There are several 'layers' of things you might reflect on throughout the project, and at the end – some of these are shown in Figure 11.1.

Thinking individually, you could all reflect on how you came into the project, why and how this was shaped by your personal history and life experiences. Reflections across the team could look at how well you are working/have worked together, who you are as a research team and what you have achieved together. Reflections on the research topic could include what you now know and how your understanding of it has shifted. Thinking about the process, we might reflect on how each stage of research is going/went, which were enjoyable or not and why and what you might do differently. The possibilities for questions are almost endless!

This might be a discussion for team development, or it might be something you want to record and report back as part of the research. Either way, you will all need to decide which of these questions are most important and work out how you might collect the team's reflections on them. Perhaps a discussion will work, or you might consider doing something more creative.

Figure 11.1: Layers of reflection on research

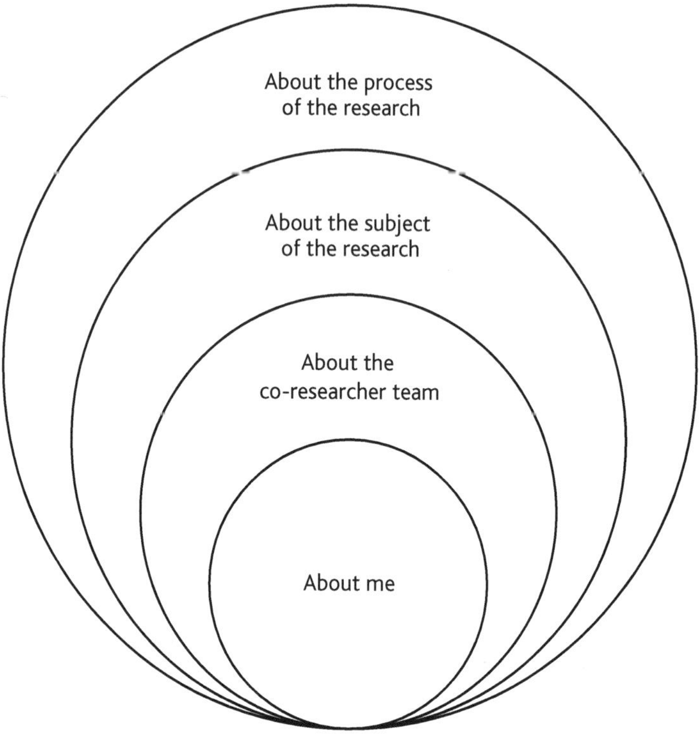

Hopefully you will have created some change or 'impact' through the research. It is really useful to review the different changes that have occurred. This is perhaps a discussion around who things have changed for and what the change was. Here's some of our ideas:

Who have changes happened for?

- The research team
- Community members
- The community
- Practitioners who serve the community
- Organisations who serve the community
- Services for the community
- Local governance of the community

What changes have happened?

- Development of skills, confidence, knowledge for community members;
- involvement of people who may not usually be active participants in research;
- research questions are more relevant to community than would have been otherwise;
- new social relationships, trust and collaborations;
- communities feeling empowered;
- increased acceptance of research findings;
- improvements to communities, services, resources;
- improved social justice in community/wider society.

Reviewing the changes throughout, as well as at the end of the research project, are important celebratory moments. You and the team of co-researchers will have invested significant time and energy into the project, and it is important to celebrate what has been achieved, reinforcing people's sense of achievement and personal capability.

Quality measures: evaluating 'how good' your participatory research is

Quality measures refer to how we will work out how good the research is throughout the process and at the end. We might judge the quality of a cup of tea by how much someone enjoys it or how many people buy it. But how do we work out the quality of research?

Different types of research have different types of measures. For example, quantitative research will look for large participant numbers, and statistical measures of validity for a quality measure. But those are not important in this social participatory space. Agreeing with Springett and colleagues (2016) we propose the following measures of quality which are directly related to the aims of participatory research:

1. Participation: to what extent was everyone able to participate to the level they wanted?

2. Relational: to what extent was everyone able to work together to achieve the research goal?

3. Ethical: to what extent did the research process keep everyone safe, and to what extent did it support ethical goals, such as the greater involvement of people usually excluded from research?

4. Community-orientated: to what extent did the community drive the research agenda, and how much have they benefited from the research?

5. Power shifting: to what extent was the research able to level power imbalances and to what extent did it increase the power of co-researchers and participants?

6. Capacity building and co-learning: to what extent did the co-researchers and participants learn and gain skills through the process?

7. Action-orientated: to what extent did the research bring about actions to increase equity?

8. Rigour: how thorough was the research process, and how confident are the community that it represents them?

9. Meaningful: how rich and meaningful do the co-researchers and community feel the findings are?

10. Social change: to what extent did the project bring about change for themselves, locally or nationally?

You will notice that many of these quality measures overlap with the reflective points previously discussed. This is intentional. As we noted above, it's important to reflect and evaluate throughout the project in order to influence change during (process) and as a result (outcome). Often reflections throughout will enrich any evaluation at the end. You and the co-researchers could use all ten quality measures or choose those that are most important to you all. Reflecting on each, you will all get a sense of the extent to which the research was participatory and contributed to individuals and communities' lives.

The process should not gloss over issues or hide areas of weakness, but there should be a discussion where you can hold yourselves to account, draw out learning points for the future and celebrate the successes you have had. It is important that we are transparent about what we do in participatory research. When talking or writing about our research to other people it can be really tempting to gloss over the issues and the difficulties; to sweep the mess under the carpet. Indeed, most research reports and papers do just that. This does not help other participatory teams to manage the research process though, and it can hide important learning points. We'll draw again here from Jo Aldridge (2016: 154) who states 'what is missing from many studies that make participatory claims, is recognition of the nature, extent and limitations of participation within individual projects'.

You may also wish to add these reflections into a section on quality measures and the strengths and limitations of the research into any output you share with other people.

Applying a social justice lens to the evaluation of the project

Throughout this book we have advocated for participatory research as a way to bring about greater equality and equity in the world, and how it can increase social justice. It is therefore important that we apply principles of social justice to the review and evaluation of participatory projects. There are two main ways in which to tackle this.

The first is to conduct the evaluation in a socially just manner – you may wish to open up the review conversation to include different stakeholders. How would the wider participants respond to the ten questions? What would the community say? How would local politicians or managers of services respond? You would then bring all these different views together to understand who thought the project was good or otherwise, why and what that might mean for future local participatory research projects.

A second way to align your project to the goal is to explicitly ask about it. Whilst question ten asks about social change, it could be focused further in an eleventh question asking: to what extent has this project increased or decreased equality and equity, for whom and in what ways? This is a challenging question but could lead to rich discussion and perhaps even a new research project!

Reflective task and tea break eleven

How socially just were you?

This chapter has encouraged you to review with the co-researchers collaboratively. But now is an opportunity for you to reflect on how well you have got on supporting this group to run their own research project. Consider:

- What was your starting point – was this your idea or a community idea?
- How did you invite people in, how equal and equitable was this?
- How have you sustained trusting and respectful relationships in the project?
- How much have you influenced the project decisions or not?
- What would you do the same in the future, and what would you change?
- Where did your power play out and how did you manage it?
- How satisfied were you with the process and outcome of the research?

- What have you learned through this participatory project?
- How might you support other groups or communities to start their own participatory research projects?

Summary

This chapter has given you a range of different ideas to think about when delivering a participatory research project. A range of tips have been provided to help you plan the delivery of the research project as a team, as well as to help the team work together and to overcome problems that may arise. It is important to reflect on and review or evaluate the success of your project throughout, as well as at the end, and this chapter proposes quality measures for this.

Further reading

- Maria Elena Torre poses some really interesting questions to ask throughout a participatory action research project in the table near the bottom of this website: https://participatoryact ionresearch.sites.carleton.edu/about-par/
- Pain, R., Askins, K. and Banks, S. (2015) *Mapping Alternative Impact: Alternative Approaches to Impact from Co-Produced Research*, Durham: Centre for Social Justice and Community Action.
- These books provide an interesting overview of research and social change: Jolivette, A. (2015) *Research Justice. Methodologies for Social Change*, Bristol: Policy Press; Cornwall, A. (2011) *The Participation Reader*, London: Zed Books.
- This film offers and introduction to coaching: https://www.youtube.com/watch?v=kbOVHbzq5Go
- And here you can find a guide to project management: https://www.youtube.com/watch?v=ZWmXi3TW1y
- This YouTube video gives some useful tips on reflective practice: https://www.youtube.com/watch?v=iBmt H0Qx0YU

Conclusion

Chapter overview

This concluding chapter revisits the key characteristics of participatory research and links them with wellbeing and social justice in order to give you a framework within which to create positive social change with communities.

Revisiting the principles of participatory research

Participatory research is grounded in assumptions that are radically different to many other forms of research. This is one reason why it happens relatively rarely. It is also comparatively lengthy to undertake, complex and resource intensive. However, it is also highly rewarding and worthwhile – for us, this far outweighs the challenges.

Let's revisit some of the central assumptions behind participatory research in Table C.1 to remind ourselves of why it is such a powerful form of research. These are very stark examples to exemplify the point rather than to critique other forms of research which are all valuable in their own right, but different to participatory research.

Table C.1: Revisiting the principles of participatory research

Participatory research focuses on ...	Where other research tends to focus on ...	... and so what?
People with lived experience of the research issues in the communities they influence: A subjective and power-sharing approach	Positioning people as the objects of research with no power or choices in the process: An objective power-holding approach	The people experiencing the issues are most likely to know how to generate the best knowledge about those issues
Valuing everyone's knowledge and skills	Valuing the researchers' knowledge and skills	Everyone brings their skills together to make the research more meaningful
Including a wide range of methods, tools and forms of knowledge defined by the people involved	Using a narrow range of tools and certain forms of knowledge defined by the researcher	Knowledge is created in more democratic ways, not just by the powerful elite
Deliberately sharing as much power as possible and seeking to support the empowerment of people involved	Researchers holding the power and carefully controlling the project	Involvement in the projects can lead to improved outcomes for the people involved
Seeking opportunities for mutual learning and critical consciousness	Providing no intentional opportunities for learning or development	Both the researchers and those with lived experience learning together
Being ethically concerned with protecting people involved from harm and honouring their contributions	Being ethically concerned with protection from harm	Everyone is credited with involvement wherever possible
Being committed to creating social justice and taking political action	Being committed to the publication of researcher knowledge	It is an active form of research committed to change for the benefit of society

These principles mean that a participatory research project is about far more than finding something out. It is committing to a community-led inquiry; it is about learning with people and about people; it is a complex process of change and development. It is fundamentally about making the world a better place. We hope you think those are worthy goals and that this book has given you the inspiration to give it a go.

Participatory research, wellbeing and social justice

We (Kaz and Lucy) have a longstanding commitment to wellbeing development. By this we mean feeling good and functioning well (Aked et al., 2008). We are deeply committed to supporting people's wellbeing. We know we cannot do wellbeing to people; we can only provide the conditions in which they can work towards their own wellbeing. This is limited by social justice and the contexts in which they live. These contexts are not equal or equitable, many people are born into less favourable contexts than others and this can shape their lifelong opportunities for wellbeing. For us, wellbeing and context (and therefore, social justice) interact with one another. Context affects wellbeing, but wellbeing also affects context and social justice: the better someone can feel and can function, the more they can do to improve the contexts in which they live. These mutually reinforcing factors affect one another as shown in the outer ring of Figure C.1.

The contexts people live in are full of structures (shown in the middle ring of Figure C.1). These include structures such as laws, social expectations, norms, family rules, resources available and so on. These can either enable or constrain someone depending on how favourable they are. These structures then affect how much agency someone has. Agency is someone's ability to be aware of what they want and to take actions to achieve those goals. Agency is therefore affected by the structures we live in and also can change the structures. We need only look back to recent history to see how agentic people have been in the Black Lives Matter campaigns despite centuries of oppressive structures. So structure and agency sit in relationship with one another within wellbeing and social justice. The more agency one has, the more likely they are to have higher levels of wellbeing.

At the heart of this model is empowerment. Someone who is empowered has a good awareness of themselves, others and their context, and so they make choices in line with their goals and take actions to achieve them. Wellbeing development, for us, is therefore committed to supporting the empowerment of people by providing opportunities for them to increase their awareness, to make choices and to act. This is shown in the centre of the diagram below.

Increasing awareness, choice and actions are central premises in participatory research. For us, participatory research is therefore a fundamental process in wellbeing development, with the potential to affect profound social change. We hope this wider context for running participatory research is as motivating for you as it is for us.

We are living in unprecedented times, facing challenges on a local and global scale. Problems seem complex or 'wicked' (Grint, 2008) and it would appear that academics generating knowledge, and privileged power holders making decisions, are not going to move humanity out of crisis. We suggest participatory research will

Figure C.1: The wellbeing and social justice model

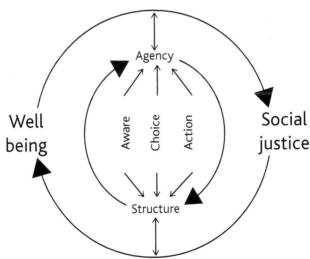

Source: Maynard and Stuart (2018)

not only change the way society produces and values knowledge, but also equip communities with the skills to be active citizens and to effect positive change. We are surrounded by examples of community movements, such as 'Me Too', 'Black Lives Matter' and 'Extinction Rebellion', to tackle issues. The skills and empowerment that come with participatory research can add further to community movements and effect change. Never has this been so needed. Every time you research with someone into a local issue to improve the lives of a few people you are contributing to that greater global good and we wish you well in all your endeavours.

References

Aked, J., Marks, N., Cordon, C. and Thompson, S. (2008) *Five Ways to Well-being*, London: New Economics Foundation.

Aldridge, J. (2016) *Participatory Research. Working with Vulnerable Groups in Research and Practice*, Bristol: Policy Press.

Banks, S. and Brydon-Miller, M. (2018) *Ethics in Participatory Research for Health and Wellbeing*, Abingdon: Routledge.

Bell, P. (2000) 'Content analysis of visual images', in T. Van Leeuwen and C. Jewitt (eds) *The Handbook of Visual Analysis*, London: Sage, pp. 10–34.

The Community Alliance for Research and Engagement (2021) 'Beyond scientific publication: strategies for disseminating research findings', Available at: https://www.idaea.csic.es/sites/default/files/CARE-Beyond-Scientific-Publication-Strategies-for-Disseminating-Research-Findings.pdf

Cook, T. (2009) 'The purpose of mess in action research: Building rigour though a messy turn', *Educational Action Research*, 17: 277–91, doi:10.1080/09650790902914241

Flicker, S., Travers, R., Guta, A., McDonald, S. and Meagher, A. (2007) 'Ethical dilemmas in community-based participatory research: recommendations for institutional review boards', *Journal of Urban Health*, 84(4): 478–93, doi: 10.1007/s11524-007-9165-7

Grint, K. (2008) 'Wicked problems and clumsy solutions: the role of leadership', Stockport: BAMM Publications.

Lundy, P. and McGovern, M. (2006) 'The ethics of silence. Action research, community 'truth telling' and post-conflict transition in the North of Ireland', *Action Research*, 4(1): 49–64.

Maguire, P. (2014) 'Feminist Participatory Research', in A. Jaggar (ed.) *Just Methods – An Interdisciplinary Feminist Reader*, Abingdon: Routledge, pp. 417–31.

Mannay, D. (2016) *Visual, Narrative and Creative Research Methods*, London: Routledge.

Maynard, L. and Stuart, K. (2018) *Promoting Young People's Wellbeing Through Empowerment and Agency: A Critical Framework for Practice*, London: Routledge.

National Institute for Health Research (2021) 'Payment guidance for researchers and professionals', Available at: https://www.nihr.ac.uk/documents/payment-guidance-for-researchers-and-professionals/27392

Office for National Statistics (2021) 'Surveys using our four personal well-being Questions', Available at: https://www.ons.gov.uk/peoplepopulationandcommunity/wellbeing/methodologies/surveysusingthe4officefornationalstatisticspersonalwellbeingquestions

Schubotz, D. (2019) 'Participatory action research', in P. Atkinson, S. Delamont, A. Cernat, J. Sakshaug, and R. Williams (eds), *SAGE Research Methods Foundations*, London: Sage, https://doi.org/10.4135/9781526421036

Springett, J., Atkey, K., Kongats, K., Zulla, R. and Wilkins, E. (2016) 'Conceptualizing quality in participatory health research: a phenomenographic inquiry', *Forum Qualitative Sozialforschung [Forum: Qualitative Social Research]*, 17(2): https://doi.org/10.17169/fqs-17.2.2568

Statista (2020) 'Annual per capita tea consumption worldwide', Available at: https://www.statista.com/statistics/507950/global-per-capita-tea-consumption-by-country/

Stuart, K., Maynard, L. and Rouncefield, C. (2015) *Evaluation Practice for Projects with Young People: Creative Research Methods*, London: Sage.

Index

Note: References to figures appear in *italic* type;
those in **bold** type refer to tables.